LAW OF THE LAND

A Practical Legal Guide for Tourists and Business Travelers

Australia

By Michael L. Moore Esq.

DEDICATION

This book is dedicated to the memory of my late older brother, Kenneth Lee Moore, whose tragic murder at 15 years of age inspired me to write this series of books.

This book is also dedicated to my parents, John Henry Moore, and Edna Mae Moore, whose tremendous parenting skills kept me focused on the important things in life: being reverent, getting educated, and prioritizing family.

Finally, this book is dedicated to my beautiful family, my wife Royellen, my son AJ, and my daughter Karla. They inspire me every single day to be kind, patient, and compassionate.

IN LOVING MEMORY OF:

Belinda Joyce Moore Moss—my beautiful and wonderful sister, who supported me in every positive thing that I ever attempted to do.

Michael Eugene Baker—my dedicated and loyal friend and brother, who always wanted the very best for me.

Sylvia Joyce Hill—my eldest sister, who had a beautiful spirit and was like a second mother to me.

LAW OF THE LAND®
PUBLISHING for Tourists & Business Travelers

Travel smart. Stay legal. Stay safe.®

From local laws to medical guides we've got you covered world wide
in one digital platform.

Travel Safe Anywhere
3 MONTHS FREE TRIAL

SCAN QR code
for more info

PREFACE

My introduction to the justice system came when I was only 10 years old. My 15-year-old brother was murdered with a butcher knife by a 19-year-old in a simple argument over a torn shirt. I was devastated by his death and sought retribution for his fate that never came. The woman was initially charged with second degree murder, but after plea negotiations, she was convicted of manslaughter and sentenced to only five years in a youthful offender school and ordered to undergo psychiatric care. That was it. Nothing more. The judicial system had run its course.

My family knew nothing about the justice system, and we did not have the tools to advocate for ourselves. No one provided us with a written source to reference for guidance through this process. There was no easily accessible, easy to understand, definitive source to educate ourselves about the legal system that we suddenly and unexpectedly found ourselves immersed in after being victimized by such a violent criminal act.

As I got older, finished college, law school, and ultimately started practicing law, it became clear to me that most people are not knowledgeable about the law or how the judicial process works. If most people are uninformed here in the United States regarding the law and the legal process, how would they fare when in other countries? I realized that tourists and businesspeople who travel internationally needed access to information on how to navigate the legal system in other countries!

For many years, there has been considerable media attention focused on international travelers experiencing legal difficulties while traveling abroad. Most of these news stories gained attention in the United States and abroad because they involved American citizens facing punishment that was considered "unconventional" and "harsh" by United States' legal standards. I recall a news story in 1994 regarding Michael Fay, a young American male, who had broken the law in Singapore. He was convicted and sentenced to be caned and or whipped publicly. While the United States Government weighed in on the inappropriate and cruel nature of the punishment, the young American was beaten because he had been convicted under Singapore law.

Similarly, in recent years, international news stories have garnered headlines regarding foreign travelers and their issues with the laws of countries that were not their own. Amanda Knox, an American woman, was accused of murdering her roommate in Italy in 2007 and spent almost four years in an Italian prison before being definitively acquitted by the Supreme Court of Cassatio. Kenneth Bae, an American citizen, was arrested in North Korea in 2012 and was convicted for hostile acts against the communist country. He was sentenced to 15 years hard labor but was released in 2014 after efforts by the U.S. State Department. More recently, United States Basketball Star, Brittany Griner was arrested in February 2022 at a Moscow airport on drug-related charges and detained for nearly 10 months, spending much of that time in prison. Her plight unfolded at the same time Russia invaded Ukraine and further heightened tensions between Russia and the United States, ending only after she was freed in exchange for a notorious Russian arms dealer.

It was in 1994 that another personal tragic event occurred that finally inspired me to write these series of books. A dear friend and also client of mine was brutally murdered while on his second honeymoon in Jamaica. News of his murder shocked me and our local community. The legal hurdles his family had to overcome to see that justice was properly dispensed far away from home, in another country, with an entirely different set of criminal procedural rules and laws, was difficult to navigate.

As I was my friend's attorney at the time of his death, his family asked that I act as their "legal liaison" to the Jamaican Prosecutor's Office and to the Jamaican Police Department. I participated in multiple police interviews with my client's widow because she was the primary witness to his murder. As a former prosecuting attorney, I was also allowed by the Court, as a professional courtesy, to sit at the prosecutor's table to consult with the prosecuting attorney during trial. What I observed about the Jamaican trial process from a front row seat was compelling enough to cause me to seriously consider educating the "world" regarding what to expect and how to act appropriately when faced with legal issues while traveling abroad.

One of the realities in life is that, regardless of what country you are in, it is never a pleasant experience to run afoul of the law and be forced to accept that someone else will be making a decision about your pecuniary, proprietary, or penal interests (your money, your property, or your freedom).

It is important to know what the laws are, how they apply to you, and how to navigate the legal system if you are charged with a crime. It is also very helpful to know what resources are available to you if you are the victim of a criminal act. At the end of the day, an "ounce of prevention is worth a pound of cure," so the more knowledge you have, the more ammunition you possess, and the more likely you will have a positive outcome.

If you are traveling to Australia, the first thing you should pack is a copy of this book! The helpful information and tips contained in this volume will provide a great starting point for knowing what to do (and not to do!) when you arrive at your destination and will help ensure that you have a wonderful vacation or business trip unmarred by tangles with the law.

TABLE OF CONTENTS

INTRODUCTION

INTRODUCTION

As a practicing attorney for over 34 years, I have encountered numerous clients who travel often, but are unaware of the laws of the land they are traveling to.

Therefore, many years ago, I decided to write a series of books that would explain the laws of specific countries. My focus was to explain the laws that may affect travelers in a straightforward manner, without all of the legal language that is sometimes hard for even seasoned attorneys to understand.

About This Book

The aim of this book is simple. It provides you, the traveler, with a simple, easy to read book that will provide a basic legal guide that explains the law in the country that you are about to visit. It is not intended to educate you on ALL of the laws in a given country. The goal is to provide you with the details of the most common legal and safety issues faced by tourists and business travelers.

I have also provided context with background information on places not to visit, statistics on the country and prevention measures you should take to safeguard your legal and physical safety. Knowledge is a powerful thing and knowing how to stay out of trouble (or how to get out of it!) is important for everyone who travels.

This *Law of The Land/Australia* book simply helps you become more informed about your legal rights, responsibilities, and obligations in a wide range of subject areas.

Last, but not least, this book does NOT purport to offer legal advice. It does, however, provide the information you need to stay safe, follow the law and navigate around legal difficulties. However, if you do face legal difficulties, the information in this book will provide you with a starting point for solving the problem and obtaining legal assistance should it be required.

Hypotheticals Used Throughout This Book

From time to time throughout this book, I will explain the law to readers by using hypothetical scenarios. These hypotheticals will be marked by an icon that will be explained in further detail as you read on.

How This Book is Organized

CHAPTER 1: **About Australia.** This chapter will provide you with a brief overview about Australia and its history. It also addresses Visa requirements, monetary advice, and the best times to visit.

CHAPTER 2: **Customs.** This chapter will provide information on what to expect when entering Australia. It will also explain what restricted and prohibited items are when entering Australia along with custom's regulations.

CHAPTER 3: **Crime in Australia.** This chapter provides an overview of the history of crime in Australia and steps that Australia's officials have taken to curb the high rate of crime.

CHAPTER 4: **Criminal Law Violations.** This chapter will provide information on drug offenses, penalties, true events and questions and answers.

CHAPTER 5: **Alcohol-Related Offenses.** This chapter will provide key points regarding the sale, consumption, and regulations of alcohol use in Australia.

CHAPTER 6: **Firearm & Ammunition Offenses.** This chapter will provide key points regarding the possession of firearms and ammunition in Australia.

CHAPTER 7: **Prostitution.** This chapter provides an overview of the history of prostitution in Australia, laws and penalties, prostitution practices, sex trafficking, sex tourism, health in Australia, tips to avoid being hassled, a Law of the Land Hypothetical, and the current situation on prostitution in Australia.

CHAPTER 8: **LGBTQ.** This chapter will provide information regarding the acceptance of LGBTQ people in Australia and the laws surrounding homosexuality.

CHAPTER 9: **Sexually Motivated/Violent Crimes.** This chapter will provide an overview of sexually related crimes in Australia.

CHAPTER 10: **Arrested in Australia.** This chapter will provide information on what to do if you are arrested in Australia.

CHAPTER 11: **Jails vs. Prisons: Conditions & Culture.** This chapter will provide information on the conditions and culture of Australia's Jails and Prisons.

CHAPTER 12: **Helping a Friend or Relative Imprisoned in Australia.** This chapter will provide information on how you can assist a friend or relative imprisoned in Australia.

CHAPTER 13: **The Administration of Justice.** This chapter will provide information on Australia's Legal System.

CHAPTER 14: **Crime Victim Assistance.** This chapter will provide information on crime victim assistance along with providing safety tips.

CHAPTER 15: **Police.** This chapter will provide information on the Australian Police and how to report a crime.

CHAPTER 16: **How to Get Legal Help in Australia.** This chapter will provide information regarding how to obtain legal assistance for travelers to Australia.

CHAPTER 17: **Medical Facilities & Hospitals.** This chapter will provide information about how to obtain medical care while visiting Australia.

CHAPTER 18: **Driving in Australia.** This chapter will provide information on driving in Australia, it's traffic rules, and road safety tips.

CHAPTER 19: **Nude Beaches & Clothing-Optional Resorts.** This chapter will provide an overview of nude beaches and clothing-optional resorts in Australia, and the legality and safety of visiting nude beaches in Australia.

CHAPTER 20: **Unusual Laws.** This chapter will provide information on some Unusual Laws in Australia, and penalties and fines.

CHAPTER 21: **Traveling Safely.** This chapter will provide information on women traveling alone, crime prevention for families, safety notes for all travelers, and overall advice.

CHAPTER 22: **Tourist Taxation.** This chapter will provide information on taxes that tourists are required to pay in Australia.

CHAPTER 23: **Long-Term Stays.** This chapter will provide an overview of the consequences for overstaying your visit to Australia.

CHAPTER 24: **Civil Litigation.** This chapter will provide information about the civil litigation process in Australia.

CHAPTER 25: **Other Things to Know.** This chapter will provide information on the harassment of tourists, travel and safety, and other practical tips.

CHAPTER 26: **Quick Reference Guide.** This chapter is a quick way to get information. It is a condensed version of the chapters in this book.

Emergency/Important Contact Numbers in Australia

Useful Aussie Slang Phrases

Glossary

Icons Used in this Book

What do those pictures throughout the book mean? See below:

WARNING: This icon flags information about things you should **avoid** while visiting Australia. Heed the advice next to this icon to avoid legal perils.

REMEMBER: This icon flags noteworthy information that you **shouldn't forget.**

HELPFUL TIPS: This icon flags information that will help you when entering Australia, relates to a legal situation, or refers to resources available while visiting Australia.

TECHNICAL INFORMATION: This icon flags technical aspects of the law. If you are faced with a legal problem, and you want to learn more about the law involved, this information can be helpful.

 **ADDITIONAL INFORMATION**: This icon points to the location of additional information available on the internet.

 **HYPOTHETICAL**: This icon points to hypothetical scenarios to illustrate possible legal problems and the outcome.

 **QUESTIONS**: This icon points to questions and answers throughout the book.

 **TRUE STORY**: This icon points to true events throughout the book.

Where to Go From Here

If you have a specific question about the law in Australia as it relates to a particular area, just turn to the chapter that addresses that issue, or turn to the Quick Reference Guide. You can also read the book from cover to cover to obtain a more comprehensive understanding of Australian laws and resources available should you find yourself in a legal predicament while visiting.

 **Disclaimer:** While the recommendations in this book primarily address U.S. citizens, the information is relevant and applicable to citizens of any country.

ABOUT AUSTRALIA

- About Australia
- Australia, the Basics
- Australian Hospitality

ABOUT AUSTRALIA

About Australia

Australia is located in the Southern Hemisphere between the Indian and Pacific Oceans. It is the world's **sixth-largest country by land area**, covering approximately **7.7 million square kilometers (2.97 million square miles)**. It is both **a continent and a country** and is geographically isolated, contributing to its unique biodiversity. As of 2023, Australia has a population of about **26.8 million people**, with the majority living along the eastern and southeastern coasts.

Australia is made up of **six states** and **ten territories**, each with its own unique geography, governance, and role within the federation. The six states—**New South Wales, Victoria, Queensland, South Australia, Western Australia, and Tasmania**—form the core of the nation. These states were once separate British colonies and became states when they federated in 1901. Each one has its own government, laws, and constitution, giving them a high degree of autonomy in areas like education, transport, and health. For example, New South Wales, with Sydney as its capital, is Australia's most populous state, while Western Australia covers an immense land area with **Perth** as its remote capital on the Indian Ocean.

Beyond the states, Australia includes ten territories. Two of these, the **Northern Territory** and the **Australian Capital Territory**, are located on the mainland and have a degree of self-governance, though not as extensive as the states. The Northern Territory, with its capital in **Darwin**, is known for its outback landscapes and indigenous heritage. The Australian Capital Territory, home to **Canberra**, is the seat of the federal government. It was carved out of New South Wales specifically to host the nation's capital.

The remaining eight territories are mostly external and scattered across the ocean, often small in size and population. These include places like **Norfolk Island, Christmas Island, and the Cocos (Keeling) Islands**, which lie far from the mainland and are directly administered by the federal government. Other territories, like the remote and uninhabited Heard Island and McDonald Islands or the expansive but icy Australian Antarctic Territory, serve more strategic or scientific purposes than civilian life.

Australia's division into states and territories reflects its colonial history and practical needs for governance across a large and diverse landscape. While the states operate with considerable independence, the territories—especially the external ones—remain more directly under federal control, showing a layered system that balances national unity with regional identity.

Australia is well known for its **stunning natural landscapes**, from the Great Barrier Reef and Uluru to vast deserts, rainforests, and pristine beaches. It is home to unique wildlife like kangaroos, koalas, and wombats. Australia is also famous for its relaxed lifestyle, Aboriginal heritage, multicultural society, and outdoor culture. The country has a strong sporting tradition (notably in cricket, rugby, and surfing), world-class wine regions, and iconic cities like Sydney and Melbourne.

Australia has been inhabited for over 65,000 years by the Aboriginal and Torres Strait Islander peoples, making it home to the world's oldest continuing cultures. European exploration began in the 17th century, but it was **the British** who established **a penal colony** in 1788 in present-day Sydney. Over time, more colonies were established, and in 1901, Australia became a federated nation, known as the **Commonwealth of Australia**, with its own constitution and parliament. The country participated in both World Wars, aligned with Britain and later the United

States. Post-WWII immigration transformed Australia into a multicultural society. Today, it is a **stable, high-income democracy**, a member of the **United Nations, Commonwealth**, and **OECD**, with a high quality of life and strong global connections.

The Capital

The capital of Australia is **Canberra**, located in the Australian Capital Territory (ACT) between the major cities of Sydney and Melbourne. It was purpose-built and officially became the capital in 1913 as a compromise between the two rival cities. Canberra is the center of Australia's political life, home to the **Parliament House, High Court**, and numerous national institutions such as the **National Gallery, Australian War Memorial**, and **National Library**. Unlike other capitals, it has a spacious, planned layout with abundant green space and a slower pace of life.

The People

Australians, or "Aussies," are known for their **laid-back attitude**, strong sense of **fairness and equality**, and **outdoor lifestyle**. The country is **culturally diverse**, shaped by waves of immigration from Europe, Asia, and the Pacific. About 30% of Australians were born overseas, contributing to a rich mix of languages, cuisines, and customs.

Australia also has a growing awareness of and respect for **Indigenous cultures**, although challenges remain around reconciliation and social equity. National holidays like **Australia Day** (January 26) and **NAIDOC Week** recognize both colonial and Aboriginal histories.

Language

The official language of Australia is **English**, spoken with a distinctive Australian accent. English is used in education, media, and government. Due to its multicultural population, over **300 languages** are spoken in Australian homes, including Mandarin, Arabic, Cantonese, Vietnamese, and Italian.

Australia also recognizes and supports **Aboriginal languages**, though many are endangered. Bilingual education programs exist in some communities, and there's a growing effort to preserve and revitalize Indigenous tongues.

Religion

Australia is a **secular country** with religious freedom. As of the 2021 census, around **38% of Australians identify with no religion**, making it the largest category. Christianity remains the largest religious group (about 44%), with **Catholicism** and **Anglicanism** being the most common denominations.

There are also growing communities of **Islam**, **Buddhism**, **Hinduism**, and **Judaism**, reflecting Australia's immigration patterns. While religion plays a lesser public role than in many other countries, it continues to influence community values and cultural traditions.

Affordability

Australia is considered a **relatively expensive** country by global standards, particularly in its major cities. **Sydney** and **Melbourne** often rank among the world's priciest cities, especially for housing and dining. However, quality of life, public healthcare, and wages are generally high.

- **Accommodation:** A night in a mid-range hotel can cost **$100–$160 USD**, while hostels may range from **$25–$40 USD**. Airbnb and vacation rentals are also popular and widely available.

- **Food:** Eating out can be costly. A basic meal at a casual restaurant might cost **$12–$20 USD**, and a coffee typically costs **$3–$4.50 USD**.

- **Transport:** Public transportation in major cities is efficient but varies by state. A one-way ticket is usually **$2.50–$4 USD**, and monthly transit passes can cost **$90–$130 USD**.

- **Attractions:** Many natural attractions are free or low-cost. Entry to museums, zoos, and cultural events can range from **$10 to $35**

USD. Tours (such as to the Great Ocean Road or the Outback) may cost **$70–$200+ USD** depending on length and inclusions.

Australia is more affordable outside major cities, especially in **regional towns** or **smaller coastal areas**, where food and accommodation prices are lower and local culture is vibrant.

Australia, the Basics

How to Get There?

Australia is a **long-haul destination** for most travelers outside Oceania, but it is well-connected to Asia, North America, the Middle East, and Europe via major international air routes. Thanks to its strong tourism infrastructure, multiple entry points, and partnerships with global airlines, getting to Australia has become increasingly streamlined—though flights can be lengthy and relatively expensive. Strategic planning around flight times, layovers, and seasons can make travel both more affordable and convenient.

Australia's largest and busiest international airports include:

- **Sydney Kingsford Smith Airport (SYD)**: As the primary gateway to Australia, SYD is the country's busiest airport, located just 8 kilometers (5 miles) from Sydney's city center. It offers direct flights to major cities in Asia (Tokyo, Singapore, Hong Kong), North America (Los Angeles, Dallas, Vancouver), the Middle East (Doha, Dubai), and Europe (via connecting hubs). It is a key hub for **Qantas, Virgin Australia,** and **Jetstar**.

- **Melbourne Airport (MEL)**: Also known as Tullamarine Airport, MEL is a major entry point for travelers headed to southern Australia. It is a hub for domestic and international flights, with connections to Southeast Asia, the U.S., and New Zealand. **Qantas, Jetstar, Emirates**, and **Singapore Airlines** operate extensively here.

- **Brisbane Airport (BNE)**: The gateway to Queensland and the Great Barrier Reef, BNE is a growing international hub. It offers direct flights to Auckland, Tokyo, Singapore, and Los Angeles. It is an important base for **Virgin Australia**, **Qantas**, and **Air New Zealand**.

- **Perth Airport** (**PER**): Located on Australia's west coast, PER is ideal for those flying in from Africa, the Middle East, or Southeast Asia. It's a key transit hub for **Emirates, Singapore Airlines**, and **Qatar Airways**, offering nonstop routes to London, Dubai, and Jakarta.

- **Adelaide Airport** (**ADL**) **and Cairns Airport** (**CNS**): While smaller, these airports handle a mix of international and seasonal flights, particularly to and from Asia and New Zealand. Cairns is especially popular with tourists visiting the Great Barrier Reef.

Australia is served by a mix of full-service and budget airlines. Key international carriers include:

- **Qantas** (**Australia's flagship carrier, part of the Oneworld alliance**): Offers long-haul flights from the U.S., UK, Europe (via Singapore and Dubai), and Asia.

- **Virgin Australia:** Focuses more on regional routes but partners with Delta and United for international connections.

- **Jetstar:** A Qantas subsidiary and low-cost airline that serves Australia, Asia, and Oceania.

- **Singapore Airlines, Cathay Pacific, Emirates, Etihad, Qatar Airways, Japan Airlines, and ANA**: Provide extensive routes between Australia and Europe, Asia, and the Middle East.

- **Delta, United, and American Airlines:** Offer direct flights from North America, including cities such as Los Angeles, San Francisco, and Dallas.

The **cheapest times** to fly to Australia **typically fall** during the shoulder seasons. May to early June and mid-July through September offer lower airfares, especially from North America and Europe, as they fall outside major holiday periods. Avoiding Australian school holidays and U.S. holiday weekends is also key to finding good deals. **December and January** are the **most expensive** months due to Australia's summer and the Christmas holiday season. Easter and Australian spring break (September/October) can also bring higher prices.

To get the best value, travelers should book flights 2 to 4 months in advance, use flexible date search tools like Google Flights or Skyscanner, and consider flying into alternative airports like Melbourne or Brisbane, which sometimes offer lower fares than Sydney. Mid-week departures (Tuesdays and Wednesdays) are often cheaper than weekends.

When to Visit?

Australia's vast size and geographic diversity mean that the "best time to visit" can vary by region and interests. Generally, the most favorable time for travel is during the Australian spring (September to November) and autumn (March to May), when the weather is mild, the crowds are manageable, and outdoor activities are at their best across much of the country.

Weather-wise, southern Australia (including Sydney, Melbourne, and Adelaide) experiences four seasons, with warm to hot summers (December to February) and cooler winters (June to August). Northern Australia (Darwin, Cairns) has a tropical climate with two distinct seasons: wet (November to April) and dry (May to October). The dry season is ideal for exploring the Outback, the Great Barrier Reef, and national parks like Kakadu, as temperatures are cooler and skies are clear. Western Australia (Perth) enjoys a Mediterranean climate, best visited in spring or fall to avoid summer heat and crowds.

Crowd-wise, peak tourist season coincides with Australia's summer—especially December through January—when both domestic and international travel surges. This period overlaps with Australian school holidays and Christmas, leading to high prices, crowded beaches, and booked-out attractions. The winter months (June to August) are peak season for northern destinations like the Top End and the Great Barrier Reef, while being low season for cities like Melbourne and Sydney.

Off-season travel in late autumn (May) and late winter (August) can yield fewer tourists, better accommodation deals, and pleasant weather in many regions. These months are particularly good for urban travel and wine regions like the Barossa Valley or Hunter Valley, where cooler temperatures make for a cozy vineyard experience.

Activities-wise, summer is great for beach holidays, surfing, and festivals, though the heat can be intense in inland areas. Winter offers excellent skiing in the Snowy Mountains (New South Wales and Victoria), and it's also prime time for whale watching along the eastern and southern coasts. Spring is ideal for wildflower blooms in Western Australia and exploring Tasmania, while autumn brings vineyard harvests and scenic drives through changing foliage.

Australia also hosts **several world-renowned festivals and cultural events** throughout the year:

- **Sydney Festival (January):** A major celebration of arts, music, and culture held across Sydney with performances, installations, and concerts. (**https://www.sydneyfestival.org.au**)
- **Australia Day (January 26):** National holiday marked with parades, fireworks, and community events across the country.
- **Melbourne International Comedy Festival (March/April):** One of the world's biggest comedy events, drawing performers from around the globe.)
- **Vivid Sydney (May–June):** A spectacular light, music, and ideas festival that transforms the city into a glowing art installation.
- **Dark Mofo (June):** A winter solstice festival in Hobart, Tasmania, known for avant-garde art, music, and its famous nude solstice swim.
- **Splendour in the Grass (July):** Australia's premier music and arts festival, held near Byron Bay.
- **Melbourne Cup (first Tuesday in November):** A world-famous horse race dubbed "the race that stops a nation," celebrated with fashion, parties, and public events.
- **New Year's Eve (December 31):** Sydney's Harbour fireworks are among the most iconic worldwide, drawing thousands to the city for the celebration.

For a balanced trip with good weather and fewer crowds, spring (September–November) and autumn (March–May) remain the top picks. If you're chasing tropical adventures or Outback exploration, time your visit during the dry season (May–October) for the most comfortable experience.

 # Do I Need a Visa?

Most travelers need a visa or travel authorization before entering Australia. The country does not offer visas on arrival, so it's essential to apply in advance. If you're from the European Union or certain European countries, you can apply for an **eVisitor visa** (**subclass 651**), which is free and allows stays of up to three months at a time over a 12-month period. For travelers from the United States, Canada, Japan, Singapore, and a few other countries, the **Electronic Travel Authority** (**ETA**) (**subclass 601**) is the best option. It allows multiple entries of up to three months per visit within a year and costs **AUD $ 20** (about $13 USD). Those who are not eligible for an ETA or eVisitor, or who plan to stay longer, can apply for a **Visitor visa** (**subclass 600**). This option permits visits of up to three, six, or twelve months and starts at AUD $ 190 (about $125 USD).

All visas must be secured **prior** to travel. You'll need a valid passport and may be asked to provide additional information related to health or character, depending on the type of visa and your country of origin. Visa applications are generally processed quickly, but applying well in advance is highly recommended. For personalized recommendations and eligibility, the Australian government provides an official Visa Finder tool at **https://immi.homeaffairs.gov.au/visas/getting-a-visa/visa-finder**.

How to Get Around

Getting around Australia is relatively easy, though the country's vast size means long-distance travel requires more planning. For covering large distances between major cities such as Sydney, Melbourne, Brisbane, Perth, and Adelaide, **flying** is the most efficient option. Domestic airlines like Qantas, Virgin Australia, Jetstar, and Rex operate frequent flights, with fares ranging from $50 to $250 USD one-way depending on the route, season, and how far in advance you book. For budget travel between cities, long-distance buses operated by Greyhound Australia and Premier Motor Service offer an economical if slower alternative to flying. Routes cover the East Coast and inland destinations, with fares from $30 to $100 USD depending on distance and timing.

Australia's **train network** is more limited than in Europe, but there are scenic long-distance routes like the Ghan (Adelaide to Darwin) and the Indian Pacific (Sydney to Perth). These are luxury rail experiences more than everyday transit, with tickets starting around $400 USD and going up significantly for sleeper cabins. For shorter regional travel, suburban rail networks in cities like Sydney, Melbourne, and Brisbane are efficient and well-connected to the metro and tram systems.

In urban areas, **public transport** is reliable and affordable. Sydney and Melbourne both have extensive networks of **trains**, **buses**, and **trams**. A one-way ticket typically costs about AUD $ 3–5 ($2–$3.50 USD), and daily or weekly passes offer better value for tourists staying longer. Payment is often handled via rechargeable smart cards like Opal (Sydney), Myki (Melbourne), or Go Card (Brisbane).

Taxis and **rideshare** services like **Uber**, **DiDi**, and **Ola** are widely available in Australian cities, though costs are generally higher than public transit. A 15-minute Uber ride in a city like Sydney or Melbourne usually costs between $15 and $25 USD, depending on traffic and time of day.

For those planning to explore national parks, coastal routes, or rural areas like the Outback or the Great Ocean Road, **renting a car** is a popular and often necessary option. Daily rental rates start around AUD $ 50–70 ($33–$47 USD), with additional costs for insurance, fuel, and one-way drop-off fees if applicable. Australians drive on the left side of the road, and international driver's licenses are accepted.

In coastal cities and island areas like Cairns, Hobart, or the Whitsundays, ferries, bike rentals, and walking trails are popular and scenic ways to get around. Most major cities also offer hop-on-hop-off sightseeing buses and guided tours that make local exploring easy and accessible for visitors.

 ## Monetary Advice

The official currency of Australia is the **Australian dollar** (**AUD $**). Exchange rates vary, but as of 2025, $1 USD typically equals around 1.45 to 1.55 AUD $. You can exchange currency at banks, airports, and currency exchange booths in major cities and tourist areas, but airport rates are usually less favorable. ATMs are widespread across Australia and often provide the most competitive exchange rates. If your debit or credit card waives foreign transaction fees, withdrawing cash directly from ATMs is usually the most cost-effective option.

Credit and debit cards are widely accepted throughout Australia, including in hotels, restaurants, shops, and even small cafés and public transportation systems. Visa and Mastercard are the most commonly accepted, while American Express is also accepted at many places, though sometimes with a surcharge. Contactless payments are popular and reliable. Still, it's smart to carry some cash, especially when visiting remote areas or markets. Be sure to notify your bank before traveling to avoid any holds due to suspicious international activity.

Australia uses only the Australian dollar, and U.S. dollars or other foreign currencies are not accepted for transactions. Some airport shops or international hotels might display prices in U.S. dollars for convenience, but you'll still be charged in AUD $.

Bargaining is not a common practice in Australia. Prices in stores, restaurants, and most markets are fixed. While haggling may occasionally happen at flea markets or second-hand stores, it's generally not expected or culturally standard, and attempts to bargain should always be polite and respectful.

Tipping in Australia is more relaxed than in North America. It is not required but is appreciated for good service. In restaurants, a tip of **5–10%** is customary if service is excellent, especially in more upscale venues. Tipping in cafés and casual spots is less common, though rounding up the bill or leaving small change is a nice gesture. Carrying small denominations is helpful for incidental tipping.

Australian Hospitality

Australia is known for its laid-back lifestyle, stunning natural landscapes, multicultural society, and friendly, welcoming people. Australians are proud of their country's diverse heritage and relaxed social culture, which is often centered around the outdoors—whether it's a backyard barbecue, a day at the beach, or cheering on a local sports team. Visitors to Australia often remark on the **casual warmth** and **inclusiveness** they experience, whether in bustling cities like Sydney and Melbourne or in the more remote Outback regions.

Australians express hospitality through their easygoing nature, humor, and generosity. It's common to be greeted with a casual "G'day" or "How ya going?" even by strangers, and people often take the time to chat, give directions, or share local tips. Inviting someone over for a drink, a meal, or a beach gathering is a typical way Australians show hospitality. They value authenticity, and while they may seem informal, this openness is part of their cultural charm. Sharing stories, laughing together, and not taking oneself too seriously are all part of the social fabric.

When it comes to manners, Australians appreciate **straightforwardness** and **humility**. Politeness is shown through small gestures like saying "please," "thank you," and "cheers" (used as a casual thanks). Holding doors open, offering a smile, and respecting personal space are all considered courteous. It's polite to offer to split the bill ("going Dutch") when dining out, unless someone specifically offers to pay. What's often considered impolite includes being overly boastful, interrupting others, or acting entitled—Australians tend to **value equality** and **mutual respect** in social interactions.

To show respect as a visitor, it's important to be open-minded and considerate of both Indigenous and contemporary Australian culture. Acknowledge the traditional custodians of the land, especially when visiting cultural sites, and approach Indigenous experiences with respect. Being punctual, especially for social and professional appointments, is appreciated. Australians **value their environment**—so respecting nature, cleaning up after yourself, and following rules in national parks or beaches goes a long way. Lastly, embracing the casual rhythm of life, engaging in friendly conversation, and showing interest in local customs will ensure you're warmly welcomed wherever you go.

CUSTOMS

- Travelers Entering Australia
- Customs Entitlements and Monetary Restrictions
- Restricted and Prohibited Items
- Five Practical Tips to Know Before You Go

CUSTOMS

Travelers Entering Australia

To enter Australia, most visitors need a **valid passport** and an **approved visa** or **electronic travel authority** (**ETA**) before arrival. The specific requirements depend on your nationality, length of stay, and purpose of visit. U.S. citizens, for example, can apply for either an **Electronic Travel Authority** (**subclass 601**) or an **eVisitor** (**subclass 651**) visa for short tourism or business visits of up to three months. Both options are electronic and must be approved before boarding your flight. You must also ensure your passport is valid for the duration of your stay, though a longer validity (at least 6 months) is recommended by many airlines.

When you land in Australia, you'll go through immigration and customs clearance. Expect to have your visa electronically verified, your passport scanned, and potentially be asked questions about your travel plans, accommodations, or financial means to support your stay. Australia is especially strict about **biosecurity laws** to protect its unique ecosystem. **You must declare all food, animal products, plants, and outdoor gear** (like hiking boots or camping equipment) that might carry soil or seeds. Items that are not declared or improperly declared can result in heavy fines; the incoming passenger card that you fill out before arrival includes questions about these items.

You may also be randomly selected for a customs or baggage inspection, even if you declare nothing. Avoid bringing prohibited goods like fresh fruits, meat products, or live plants.

 To speed up the process and avoid fines, consult **Australian Border Force** at **https://www.abf.gov.au/ entering-and-leaving-australia/can-you-bring-it-in**.

Customs Entitlements and Monetary Restrictions

You are allowed to carry **any amount of money** into or out of Australia, but if you bring in **AUD $10,000 (about $6,650 USD) or more (or the equivalent in foreign currency)**, you **must declare it** at customs upon arrival. This includes cash, traveler's checks, money orders, and negotiable bearer instruments. Failure to declare large sums is a criminal offense.

When entering Australia, travelers are allowed to bring specific goods through customs under **duty-free entitlements**, provided they meet the quantity and value limits. Adult travelers aged 18 and over can bring up to **2.25 liters (about 0.6 gallons) of alcoholic beverages** and **up to 25 cigarettes or 25 grams (about 0.88 ounces) of tobacco duty-free**. The total value of other personal goods—including clothing, electronics, souvenirs, and gifts—must not exceed AUD $ 900 (approximately $600 USD). For travelers under 18, the limit is AUD $450 (about $300 USD). All tobacco products, regardless of quantity, **must be declared**.

If you exceed any of the above limits, you must declare all goods, and duties and taxes will be applied to the total value, not just the excess. You may bring in prescription medication for personal **use up to a three-month supply,** but it must be declared, kept in original packaging, and accompanied by a prescription or letter from your doctor.

Restricted and Prohibited Items[1]

Australia has one of the strictest customs and biosecurity systems in the world. Many items that are commonly brought into other countries are either restricted or completely prohibited from entry into Australia due to the risk they pose to agriculture, the environment, and public safety.

Some of the most commonly prohibited or restricted items include:

- Fresh fruit and vegetables, meat, eggs, dairy, and seafood
- Seeds, nuts, grains, beans, spices, and herbal tea
- Plants, flowers, soil, and plant materials including wood or straw
- Animal products such as hides, bones, feathers, and shells
- Weapons (including pepper spray, knuckle dusters, and some knives)
- Firearms, ammunition, and firearm parts (even replicas or toys)
- Drugs and controlled substances, including certain medications without proper documentation
- Counterfeit goods and pirated media
- Pornographic material that violates Australian law (such as depictions involving violence or non-consent)

As mentioned above, there are also restrictions on bringing large amounts of alcohol and tobacco products. If these exceed duty-free allowances, you **must declare them** and pay applicable taxes.

If you're unsure whether an item is allowed, it's safer to declare it. Australia's border authorities inspect incoming luggage, use detector dogs, and conduct x-ray screenings. Failure to declare restricted or prohibited items—even unintentionally—can result in confiscation of the items, on-the-spot fines, prosecution, or a permanent note on your travel record, which could impact future entry into Australia.

---

1   https://www.abf.gov.au/importing-exporting-and-manufacturing/
     prohibited-goods/list-of-items

 A full and regularly updated list of what you can and cannot bring into Australia is available at the official **Australian Border Force** site: at **https://www.abf.gov. au/entering-and-leaving-australia/can-you-bring-it-in**.

To avoid fines or delays, always fill out your Incoming Passenger Card honestly and declare any questionable items. When in doubt, declare.

 ## Five Practical Tips to Know Before You Go

1. **Respect the Biosecurity Laws:** Australia takes biosecurity extremely seriously. When you arrive, you'll be required to declare any food, plant material, animal products, or outdoor equipment. To avoid penalties, clean your gear before flying and always declare items when in doubt.

2. **Understand the Australian Attitude:** Australians are famously laid-back, friendly, and informal, but they tend to dislike arrogance or pretension, and they value equality—so avoid flashing wealth or acting entitled. Humor, especially sarcasm, is a big part of social interaction, so don't be surprised if someone jokes with you—it's often a sign of friendliness.

3. **Know the Climate and Sun Safety:** Australia has a diverse climate ranging from tropical in the north to temperate in the south. Summer runs from December to February, and UV levels can be dangerously high—higher than most parts of the world. Always wear sunscreen, sunglasses, and a wide-brim hat, even on cloudy days.

4. **Respect Indigenous Culture:** Australia is home to the world's oldest continuous culture, with Aboriginal and Torres Strait Islander peoples. When visiting places of cultural significance show respect by learning about the history, following signage, and avoiding sacred areas

5. **Don't Underestimate the Size of the Country:** Australia is vast—about the size of the continental United States. Plan accordingly and consider flying between major cities. In rural or outback areas, always travel with enough water, fuel, and a charged phone, and let someone know your route in case of emergencies.

CRIME IN AUSTRALIA

CHAPTER 3

CRIME IN AUSTRALIA

Overview

Australia is generally considered a **safe country with relatively low crime rates**, especially compared to many other nations. The country consistently ranks high on global safety indexes; for example, the Global Peace Index 2024 placed Australia 22nd out of 163 countries, reflecting a very peaceful environment. Major cities such as Sydney, Melbourne, and Brisbane are frequently listed among the safest cities worldwide.

However, like any country, Australia does face some crime-related challenges, which vary depending on location, demographic factors, and the type of crime involved. Most crimes in Australia tend to be **non-violent**. Violent crimes, including homicide, are relatively rare, whereas **property crime**, **domestic violence**, and **cybercrime** are more common concerns.

Over the past two decades, crime rates in Australia have generally been **declining or stabilizing**, according to data from the Australian Bureau of Statistics and the Australian Institute of Criminology. The homicide rate has remained **low and stable**, averaging around 0.9 per 100,000 people in recent years. Assault rates are stable, and burglary and motor vehicle theft have significantly dropped since their peak in the late

1990s. Conversely, cybercrime and online scams have rapidly increased, especially following the COVID-19 pandemic.[2]

Several factors influence these crime trends. **Socioeconomic inequality** plays a significant role, as areas with higher unemployment, poverty, and lower education levels tend to experience more crime, particularly property and youth crime. **Substance abuse**, especially alcohol and methamphetamine, is strongly linked to domestic violence and random street assaults. **Youth disengagement** has contributed to rising youth crime in some states, particularly car theft and home invasions, often concentrated in specific regional areas such as parts of Queensland and the Northern Territory. Additionally, **technological changes**, including the increasing amount of work, shopping, and socializing conducted online, have led to a rise in cyber-enabled crimes like identity theft and online fraud.

In summary, Australia is generally a safe country, characterized by low rates of violent crime, a strong police presence, and a transparent justice system. While certain types of crime, such as cybercrime and domestic violence, are growing concerns, overall crime trends indicate stability or decline in most traditional crime categories.

Crime Hotspots in Australia

Crime hotspots in Australia are typically found in certain urban suburbs that face socio-economic challenges. In **Western Sydney**, suburbs such as **Mount Druitt, Blacktown**, and **Bankstown** report higher rates of property crime, assaults, and gang-related activity. Similarly, **Melbourne's western suburbs** like **Broadmeadows** and **Sunshine** have elevated levels of property crimes, drug offenses, and youth violence. In **Brisbane**, areas including **Inala** and **Woodridge** show higher incidences of violent crime and drug-related offenses. The **Northern Territory**, particularly **Darwin**, stands out with a comparatively high rate of violent crime, often linked to alcohol abuse and complex social issues within Indigenous communities. **Adelaide's northern suburbs**,

---

2   https://www.abs.gov.au/statistics/people/crime-and-justice

such as **Elizabeth** and **Salisbury**, also experience higher-than-average crime rates, mainly property offenses and assaults. These patterns reflect a broader trend where crime tends to cluster in economically disadvantaged neighborhoods, often driven by factors such as unemployment, drug abuse, and social disenfranchisement.

Nevertheless, Australia is considered by and large a very **safe destination for travelers**, especially when compared to the United States. Violent crime, including gun-related incidents, is rare thanks to strict firearm laws and a relatively low overall crime rate. Most urban areas and public spaces are safe, even at night, and public transportation is reliable and secure. Travelers from the U.S. are likely to find Australia to be comparably safe—or even safer—than many places at home. That said, the **main safety concerns in Australia tend to come from natural hazards rather than crime.** Visitors should be mindful of strong ocean currents at beaches, follow local warnings about wildlife, and take precautions against sun exposure and heat. However, emergency services are reliable, and the country has strong healthcare and public safety systems. As long as travelers follow basic precautions and respect local laws and customs, Australia is a safe and welcoming place to visit.

Crime Statistics

In Australia, the most common types of crime are property-related rather than violent. **Theft, burglary, vehicle break-ins**, and **fraud**—especially online scams—are the most frequently reported offenses. **Drug-related crimes** also occur, , though these tend to be concentrated in specific regions. Violent crimes such as assaults and homicides are **relatively rare** and often occur in domestic or personal contexts rather than as random acts in public spaces.

Law enforcement in Australia is generally considered **effective, professional**, and **free from widespread corruption.** Police agencies operate under strict accountability systems, and public trust in law enforcement remains high. This contributes to the country's **overall low crime rates** and makes both urban and rural areas feel secure, especially for visitors.

For tourists, the most likely risks involve **petty theft**, **pickpocketing**, or **scams**—often in crowded places like transport hubs, nightlife districts, or beaches. Occasionally, alcohol-related disturbances can occur in nightlife zones, but these are typically minor. With standard precautions, travelers will find Australia to be a very safe and welcoming country to visit.

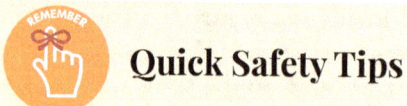

Quick Safety Tips

- **Stay Aware in Urban Hotspots:** While most areas in Australian cities are safe, exercise extra caution in known higher-crime suburbs such as Mount Druitt (Sydney), Broadmeadows (Melbourne), or Inala (Brisbane). Avoid walking alone at night in unfamiliar areas and stick to well-lit streets.

- **Be Cyber-Smart:** Cybercrime is on the rise in Australia. Use secure Wi-Fi, avoid clicking on suspicious links, and enable two-factor authentication on important accounts. Don't share personal or banking information with unfamiliar contacts, even if they appear official.

- **Secure Your Belongings:** Petty theft and pickpocketing can happen in tourist-heavy areas. Keep your bags zipped and in front of you, especially at beaches, public transport stations, or major events. Avoid leaving valuables in parked cars.

- **Be Cautious with Alcohol:** Most violent altercations in Australia occur around nightlife zones and involve alcohol. Drink responsibly, stay with friends, and avoid arguments with intoxicated individuals. In some areas, "lockout laws" may restrict late-night alcohol sales to reduce risks.

- **Respect Local Laws and Warnings:** Australia has strict laws on drugs, firearms, and public behavior. Always follow police instructions and local signage. Be especially cautious in Indigenous communities or remote areas where local customs and regulations may differ significantly from urban norms.

CRIMINAL LAW VIOLATIONS

CRIMINAL LAW VIOLATIONS

Marijuana and Other Drugs in Australia[3]

Australia has a long and evolving relationship with cannabis and other drugs. Cannabis was introduced in the 19th century, initially for industrial hemp production. Its recreational use became widespread during the 1960s and 70s, and by the late 20th century, it had become the most commonly used illicit drug in the country. In response, strict prohibition policies were enacted. Over time, however, public opinion shifted, and policies began to reflect a more health-centered, harm-reduction approach.

Medical marijuana was **legalized** at the federal level in 2016. Under this legislation, patients with conditions such as chronic pain, epilepsy, and multiple sclerosis can receive cannabis-based treatments through prescriptions from approved healthcare providers. These products are carefully regulated, and only authorized suppliers can distribute them.

Recreational cannabis, on the other hand, **remains illegal across most of Australia.** The **exception** is the **Australian Capital Territory (ACT)**, which in January 2020 became the first jurisdiction to legalize limited personal use.

---

3   https://investingnews.com/guide-to-cannabis-in-australia

Adults in the ACT can possess **up to 50 grams** of dried cannabis and grow up to two plants per person (with a household maximum of four). However, cannabis use must be private, not near children, and it is still illegal to sell, share, or consume cannabis in public. Despite local legality, federal laws continue to prohibit possession, creating a legal gray area.

Synthetic cannabinoids, often sold under names like Kronic or Spice, have posed serious public health risks in the past decade. Though they were marketed as legal alternatives to cannabis, these substances have unpredictable and sometimes life-threatening effects. As a result, **synthetic cannabinoids** were **banned nationwide** starting in 2011, and they are now listed as prohibited substances with no medical use under Schedule 9 of the Poisons Standard. Possession, manufacture, or sale can result in severe criminal penalties.

Australia's approach to other drugs remains firm, though still rooted in harm reduction. Drugs like **MDMA, cocaine, methamphetamine, heroin, and LSD** are all **illegal to possess, sell, or produce**. However, the country has taken progressive steps in some areas. In July 2023, MDMA and psilocybin (the active ingredient in magic mushrooms) were approved for very limited medical use under strict psychiatric supervision, making Australia one of the first countries to allow this.

Penalties for drug offenses **vary by state and the severity of the offense**. For small-scale cannabis possession, especially for first-time offenders, many states opt for warnings, fines (typically ranging from $200 USD to $2,000 USD), or diversion programs involving education and counseling. Larger quantities or offenses like trafficking carry significantly harsher punishments, with prison sentences that can range from several years to life, depending on the drug and the amount involved. Driving with any detectable level of THC or other illicit drugs in the system is illegal and can result in fines, license suspension, or a criminal record—even for medical cannabis patients.

For more detailed information on drug-related penalties, visit **https://www.criminallawgroup.com.au/ list-of-drug-possession-charges-and-sentences-australia/**.

Overall, drug laws in Australia are strict but increasingly nuanced. Medical cannabis is legal and tightly regulated, recreational cannabis is partially decriminalized only in the ACT, and synthetic cannabinoids and harder drugs carry serious penalties. Nonetheless, public and political attitudes are shifting, suggesting that further reforms may emerge in the future.

Prescription Medication

When traveling to Australia with prescription medication, travelers must comply with strict regulations to ensure their medicines are allowed and properly declared. Prescription medications should be **accompanied by a doctor's prescription** or a letter from a medical professional explaining the medication's purpose and dosage. It is also recommended to carry the medication in its **original packaging with clear labeling**. Certain medications, especially those containing controlled substances (like opioids, some ADHD medications, or strong sedatives), may require prior approval or an **import permit from the Australian Government's Department of Health or the Therapeutic Goods Administration (TGA).**

For over-the-counter (OTC) medications, most common drugs such as painkillers, cold and flu remedies, and allergy medications are generally allowed in reasonable quantities for personal use. However, some OTC medications that contain ingredients considered controlled substances in Australia (for example, codeine-containing products) may be restricted or require declaration and approval.

All medications **must be declared** at the Australian border upon arrival. Failure to declare prescription or controlled medications can result in penalties including fines or seizure of the medication. Bringing in medications without proper documentation or approval can lead to them being confiscated, and in some cases, travelers may face legal consequences such as fines or prosecution.

To avoid complications, travelers should check the Australian Government's official guidelines before travel, carry supporting medical documentation, declare all medications on arrival, and ensure the quantities are reasonable for personal use. This helps ensure a smooth entry process and compliance with Australian law.

 For the most up-to-date information, visit the **Australian Border Force** website at **https://www.abf.gov.au/entering-and-leaving-australia/can-you-bring-it-in/categories/medicines-and-substances**.

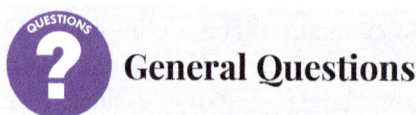 ## General Questions

1. *Is cannabis legal in Australia?* **No**. **Recreational cannabis** is **illegal** across most of Australia, except in the Australian Capital Territory (ACT), where personal use and small-scale cultivation are decriminalized but still conflict with federal law. **Medicinal cannabis** has been **legal** since 2016 with a prescription. Public support for recreational legalization is growing, but federal laws have not changed.

2. *Where can I legally purchase marijuana in Australia?* You can legally purchase cannabis in Australia **only for medicinal use** with a prescription from a registered doctor. After approval from the Therapeutic Goods Administration (TGA), prescriptions can be filled at pharmacies, though availability may be limited and costs are not subsidized. Recreational cannabis remains illegal except for personal use decriminalized in the ACT, but sales are still prohibited.

3. *Can I have marijuana on my person or in hotel room in Australia?* **No**. Possessing marijuana on your person or in a hotel room is illegal throughout Australia except in the ACT, where personal possession and cultivation are decriminalized for adults. However, using cannabis in public places, including hotel

common areas, is still prohibited everywhere. In other states, possession—even in private spaces—can lead to fines, criminal charges, or imprisonment.

4. *Are there any other exceptions to the possession and consumption of cannabis in Australia?* **No.** Aside from the Australian Capital Territory's limited decriminalization for personal use and medicinal cannabis access with a prescription nationwide, there are no other legal exceptions for cannabis possession or consumption in Australia. All other states and territories maintain strict laws prohibiting recreational cannabis use, with penalties for possession and consumption varying by jurisdiction.

5. *What are the penalties for possessing and consuming other types of illicit drugs in Australia?* Penalties for drug possession and use in Australia vary by state and drug type. Small amounts can lead to fines and up to 2 years in prison, while trafficking and large quantities carry much harsher penalties. The Australian Capital Territory has decriminalized small amounts, usually resulting in fines or health referrals, but public use remains illegal. Many states offer diversion programs for first-time offenders, focusing on rehabilitation alongside criminal penalties.

 **Law of the Land Hypothetical**

HYPOTHETICAL: *Jasmine, a 25-year-old tourist from the United States, is visiting Melbourne for two weeks. She has a valid prescription for medical cannabis issued in California, where she legally uses it for chronic pain. Before her trip, she packs a small amount in her luggage along with her prescription paperwork. Can Jasmine legally use and possess her U.S.-prescribed medical cannabis while visiting Australia?*

ANSWER: *No. While medical cannabis is legal in Australia, it must be prescribed by an Australian-registered doctor and approved through the Therapeutic Goods Administration (TGA). Jasmine's U.S. prescription is not valid under Australian law. Possessing cannabis— even for medical reasons—without proper local authorization is illegal in all states and territories, including Victoria. If found with cannabis, Jasmine could face fines, criminal charges, or even jail time, depending on the circumstances. Tourists must not bring cannabis into Australia, even with a foreign prescription. Instead, they should consult a local doctor upon arrival if they need access to medical cannabis legally.*

 ## Takeaways

- Recreational cannabis is **illegal** in all Australian states and territories except the Australian Capital Territory (ACT), where adults may possess and grow small amounts for personal use. However, it remains illegal to buy or sell cannabis for recreational purposes anywhere in Australia.

- Medical cannabis is legal nationwide but must be prescribed by an Australian doctor and approved by the Therapeutic Goods Administration (TGA). Overseas prescriptions are not recognized.

- Possessing, using, or trafficking illicit drugs—including cannabis without a prescription—can result in significant penalties, including fines, criminal charges, and imprisonment. Penalties vary by state and severity of the offense.

- Visitors bringing medications into Australia must declare them at the border and carry them in original packaging with a prescription or doctor's note. Some medications that are legal overseas may be restricted or prohibited in Australia.

- Many states offer diversion programs for first-time or low-level drug offenders, focusing on education and rehabilitation rather than jail, especially for cannabis possession.

CHAPTER 5

ALCOHOL-RELATED OFFENSES

ALCOHOL-RELATED OFFENSES

Alcohol-Related Offenses

Alcohol holds a long-standing cultural and social role in Australia. Historically, drinking has been deeply woven into Australian identity, with early colonial society centered around rum as currency and a strong pub culture emerging over time. Today, alcohol remains a common feature in social gatherings, sports events, barbecues, and holidays. While this tradition reflects a casual, sociable lifestyle, it has also contributed to some ongoing public health and safety issues related to excessive drinking.

In everyday life, alcohol consumption is widespread and often considered a normal part of socializing. It's common for Australians to meet friends at a pub after work, enjoy a glass of wine with dinner, or celebrate with a few beers during a cricket match or weekend barbecue. Drinking is socially acceptable across all age groups, though younger adults are more likely to engage in binge drinking.

Australia is known for several typical alcoholic beverages. **Beer** is especially popular. Brands like **Victoria Bitter** (**VB**), **Carlton Draught**, and **Tooheys** are local staples. The country also has a **robust wine industry**, particularly in regions like the Barossa Valley and Hunter Valley, known for producing high-quality **shiraz**, **chardonnay**, and **cabernet sauvignon**. Additionally, pre-mixed spirits and cider are widely consumed, especially among younger drinkers.

Alcohol is **legal and readily available** in Australia. It can be purchased at licensed venues such as pubs, clubs, bars, restaurants, and liquor stores. However, there are strict regulations. The **legal drinking age is 18**, and proof of age is often required. Public drinking is restricted in many areas, and each state or territory sets its own rules regarding the sale and consumption of alcohol. For example, some regions have **"dry zones"** or enforce lockout laws that limit late-night alcohol service.

Despite its legality, alcohol-related offenses are a significant concern. Common offenses include **public drunkenness**, **drink driving (DUI)**, **underage drinking, alcohol-fueled violence**, and **disturbing the peace**. Penalties can range from fines and license suspensions to jail time for repeat or serious offenses. Police frequently conduct roadside breath tests, and legal blood alcohol limits are strictly enforced. Australia's approach aims to balance its cultural embrace of drinking with public safety and harm reduction.

Alcohol Regulation

Alcohol can only be sold and consumed at licensed premises (like bars, restaurants, and liquor stores). The sale and service of alcohol are regulated by each state or territory, with strict rules about hours of operation, responsible service practices, and who may be served. It's illegal to serve alcohol to someone who is clearly intoxicated or to minors.

Alcohol advertising is regulated under a self-regulatory system called the **Alcohol Beverages Advertising Code (ABAC)**, which prohibits ads that target minors, encourage binge drinking, or suggest alcohol leads to success or enhanced performance. Advertisements are also restricted during certain television hours and in media primarily aimed at young people.[4]

Enforcement is carried out by local police, liquor licensing authorities, and health departments. Police frequently conduct **random breath**

---

4   https://www.abac.org.au/about/

testing (**RBT**) for drivers and can issue fines or make arrests for public intoxication, underage drinking, or violence linked to alcohol.

Penalties for violations include:

- **Fines** for underage possession or drinking (commonly around AUD $200-$500, or about $132 USD-$330 USD).
- **License suspensions** or bans for drunk driving (legal BAC limit is **0.05** for most drivers, **0.00** for learners/provisional).
- **Closure orders** or heavy fines for venues that break licensing laws.
- **Criminal charges** for serious offenses like drunk driving causing injury or death.

The **legal drinking age in Australia is 18**. It is illegal to buy, possess, or consume alcohol under this age unless under specific conditions, such as being in a private residence with parental consent (in some states). Selling or supplying alcohol to minors carries significant penalties for both individuals and businesses, including large fines and license revocation.

 **Things to Remember**

- **Drinking Age:** The legal drinking age across Australia is **18 years old**. It is illegal for anyone under 18 to buy, possess, or consume alcohol in public places, and supplying alcohol to minors without parental consent is also illegal.
- **ID:** You must show a valid photo ID (such as a driver's license, passport, or proof-of-age card) when purchasing alcohol, especially if you appear under 25. Licensed venues are legally required to check ID.
- **Public Consumption: Often illegal.** Drinking alcohol in public places (like streets, parks, or beaches) is banned or restricted in many areas, particularly in city centers and alcohol-free zones.

Fines may apply for carrying open containers or drinking in these zones.

- **Public Drunkenness:** Public intoxication can lead to **on-the-spot fines**, arrest, or detention in a "sobering up" facility. Penalties vary by state but typically range from **AUD $100 to $500** (about $66 USD to $330 USD) or more, depending on behavior and repeat offenses.

- **Drunk Driving:** The legal blood alcohol concentration (BAC) limit is **0.05%** for full-license holders. For learner and provisional drivers, the limit is **0.00%**. Penalties include heavy fines (over AUD $1,000, or about $660 USD), **license suspension**, demerit points, or **imprisonment** for serious/repeat offenses.

- **Purchase of Alcohol:** Alcohol can only be bought from **licensed venues** such as liquor stores (known as "bottle shops"), pubs, bars, and licensed restaurants. Sale hours vary by state but often end by **10 p.m. to midnight** for retail stores and **2 a.m. to 3 a.m.** for bars. Sunday or holiday restrictions may apply in some areas.

- **Alcohol Permits:** In some states, **a temporary liquor license or permit** may be required to serve alcohol at a public or ticketed event, especially if alcohol is being sold. Private parties generally don't need a permit unless held in a public space.

- **Illegal Alcohol:** While bootleg or homemade alcohol is **not a widespread issue** in Australia, producing or selling alcohol without a license is **illegal**. Offenders can face **fines or prosecution**.

General Questions

1. *Can I drink and drive in Australia?* **No.** Driving with a blood alcohol concentration (BAC) of **0.05% or higher** is illegal in Australia. For learner and provisional drivers, the limit is **0.00%**. Penalties include heavy fines, license suspension, and possible jail time for serious or repeat offenses.

2. ***Can I possess an open container in public?*** **No**. In many parts of Australia, possessing or consuming alcohol from an open container in public places like streets, parks, or beaches is **prohibited**. Local councils enforce alcohol-free zones, and violations can result in fines.

Law of the Land Hypothetical

HYPOTHETICAL: *Jordan, a 20-year-old American tourist, is enjoying a sunny afternoon at a public park in Sydney. He brings along a six-pack of beer and starts drinking with a few friends near a picnic area. Can someone legally drink alcohol in a public park in Australia if they are over 18?*

ANSWER: *Even though Jordan is legally allowed to drink at age 20, **public consumption of alcohol is restricted** in many parts of Australia, including public parks. Local councils often enforce **alcohol-free zones** where drinking in public spaces is prohibited, regardless of age. In Jordan's case, drinking in the park could result in a fine or confiscation of the alcohol. To avoid penalties, he should only consume alcohol in designated areas, like licensed venues or private residences.*

Takeaways

- You must be **at least 18 years old** to legally purchase, possess, or consume alcohol in Australia. Supplying alcohol to minors is strictly regulated and penalized.

- Drinking alcohol in public places—like streets, parks, or beaches— is often prohibited in designated alcohol-free zones. Violations can lead to fines or confiscation.

- The legal blood alcohol limit is **0.05%** for fully licensed drivers and **0.00%** for learners and provisional drivers. Penalties include heavy fines, license suspension, and possible jail time.

- Photo ID is mandatory when purchasing alcohol. Retailers and venues routinely check ID and can refuse service if proof is not provided.

- Alcohol can only be sold at licensed venues, and special permits may be required for events serving alcohol in public. Illegal sales or distribution are punishable by law.

FIREARM & AMMUNITION OFFENSES

FIREARM & AMMUNITION OFFENSES

Current Firearm Status and Associated Penalties

Individuals can legally own firearms in Australia, but ownership is subject to stringent regulations that vary by state and territory. The overarching framework is provided by the **National Firearms Agreement** (**NFA**), established in 1996 following the Port Arthur massacre—the worst mass shooting in modern Australian history—in which 35 people were killed and 23 others injured, prompting the implementation of some of the world's strictest gun control laws and marking a turning point in the nation's approach to firearm regulation. This agreement sets out the principles for firearm control, including licensing, registration, and safe storage requirements.

To legally own a firearm, an individual must be **at least 18 years old** and **demonstrate a "genuine reason" for ownership,** such as sport shooting, hunting, or occupational requirements like farming or pest control. Self-defense is not considered a valid reason under Australian law. Applicants must undergo **background checks**, including **criminal history** and **mental health assessments**, and complete **a firearm safety training course.** Licenses are issued by state or territory authorities and must be renewed periodically.

Firearms in Australia are categorized from A to H, with **Category A** firearms (e.g., air rifles and single-shot rimfire rifles) being the **least**

restricted, and Categories C, D, and H (e.g., semi-automatic rifles, pump-action shotguns, and handguns) being **more tightly controlled** or prohibited for civilian use. Ownership limits are imposed based on the license category and the individual's stated purpose for owning firearms.

Carrying firearms in public is **generally prohibited** unless the individual has specific authorization, such as for law enforcement or certain occupational roles. Firearms must be transported unloaded and securely stored. Using a firearm unlawfully, including for self-defense, can result in severe penalties, including imprisonment.

Recent legislative changes, particularly in Western Australia, have introduced some of the country's strictest gun laws. These include mandatory mental health checks, limits on the number of firearms an individual can own, and the establishment of a national firearms register to track firearm ownership across the country. The reforms aim to enhance public safety and ensure responsible firearm ownership.[5]

Firearm Restrictions for Visitors

Tourists and short-term visitors are **generally prohibited** from possessing, carrying, or using firearms unless they obtain a special permit in advance. These permits are rarely granted and only under specific, lawful circumstances—such as participation in approved hunting trips, competitive shooting events, or occupational duties like film production.

To legally import and possess a firearm in Australia, visitors must:[6]

1. **Obtain a Visitor's License:** Apply for a visitor's license from the police in the Australian state or territory where you intend to use the firearm. This license is typically valid for up to three months and

---

5   https://www.nraila.org/articles/20250324/
    just-one-more-step-australia-s-new-weapon-laws

6   https://www.police.qld.gov.au/weapon-licensing/
    importing-weapons-or-ammunition?utm_source

is issued only for specific purposes such as competitive shooting events or approved hunting tours.

2. **Apply for an Import Permit (B709):** Submit an application to the Australian Border Force for an import permit (B709) to bring the firearm into the country. This permit is required for all firearm imports.

3. **Meet Firearm Category Restrictions:** Only certain categories of firearms are permitted for importation. For instance, Category A and B firearms are generally allowed, while semi-automatic and fully automatic firearms are highly restricted or prohibited.

4. **Provide Supporting Documentation:** Include a copy of your passport, a valid firearms license from your home country, details of the firearm(s) you intend to bring, and any relevant event invitations or permissions from landowners if applicable.

All firearms brought into Australia **must be declared at customs**, temporarily imported under permit, and securely stored when not in use. The visitor must comply with state and territory-specific laws, and the firearm must never be carried or used outside the approved context.

Violations—such as undeclared firearms, unauthorized possession, or carrying in public—can lead to confiscation, heavy fines, detention, and even imprisonment. Australia's **zero-tolerance approach to unauthorized firearm possession** applies equally to residents and non-residents.

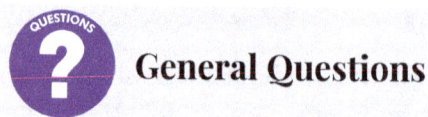

General Questions

1. *What happens if I'm caught carrying an unlicensed firearm in Australia?* If you're caught carrying a firearm in Australia without the proper license or legal authorization, you can face **serious criminal charges**, including **fines**, **arrest**, **firearm confiscation**, and **imprisonment**. Penalties vary by state and territory, but unlawful possession or carriage of a firearm is treated as a major offense, especially in public places or without valid justification.

2. *Are there any specific storage requirements for firearms brought into Australia by visitors?* Yes. Visitors bringing firearms into Australia must follow strict storage laws that vary by state. Generally, firearms must be kept in a sturdy, locked steel safe bolted to the building if under a certain weight, with ammunition stored separately. Upon arrival, firearms must be declared, and compliance with local storage rules is mandatory. Failure to follow these rules can lead to fines, firearm seizure, and criminal charges.

Law of the Land True Story[7]

In May 2023, Liliana Goodson, a 28-year-old American woman, was arrested at Sydney Airport after Australian Border Force officers discovered a 24-carat gold-plated handgun in her luggage. She had traveled from Los Angeles to attend clown school in Sydney and claimed

---

7   https://www.news.com.au/national/nsw-act/courts-law/american-woman-jailed-for-smuggling-24karat-gold-plated-gun-into-australia/news-story/17dbb30b367f325d783a105b3fbc377c?utm_source

she brought the firearm for personal protection. However, she did not possess an Australian firearms license or permit to import the weapon.

Upon questioning, Goodson initially denied carrying any prohibited items but later admitted to having the gun in her bag, stating she had "forgotten" about it. Investigations revealed she had searched online about carrying a gun in her suitcase and had set a reminder to pack it. Additionally, she had shipped 50 rounds of ammunition to Australia, which were of the wrong caliber for the handgun.

In December 2024, Goodson pleaded guilty to charges of illegally importing a prohibited firearm and ammunition. She was sentenced to 12 months in jail, with four months to be served in full-time custody. The court emphasized the need for deterrence, citing Australia's strict firearm laws and the seriousness of the offense. Goodson was also fined $1,000 USD and ordered to participate in drug counseling upon her release.

Takeaways

- Australia enforces stringent firearm regulations under the National Firearms Agreement (NFA), created after the 1996 Port Arthur massacre. Licensing, registration, background checks, and safe storage are mandatory, with self-defense not accepted as a valid reason for ownership.

- Firearms are classified by categories, with tighter restrictions or bans on semi-automatic and certain handguns. Legal owners must meet age and purpose requirements, and carrying firearms in public without authorization is prohibited.

- Tourists and visitors must obtain specific permits to bring or use firearms in Australia. These permits are rare and tightly controlled, requiring import permits, visitor licenses, and strict adherence to storage and usage rules. Unauthorized possession leads to heavy penalties.

- Unlicensed possession, illegal importation, or unauthorized use of firearms can result in fines, imprisonment, firearm confiscation, and other legal consequences. Australian authorities apply a zero-tolerance policy regardless of citizenship status.

CHAPTER 7

PROSTITUTION

IN THIS CHAPTER

- Overview
- Laws and Penalties
- Prostitution Practices
- Sex Trafficking and Exploitation
- Sex Tourism and Public Health
- Tips to Avoid Being Solicited
- Law of the Land True Story

PROSTITUTION

Overview[8]

Prostitution in Australia is **regulated differently across states and territories**, reflecting a patchwork of legal approaches. In **New South Wales** and the **Northern Territory**, prostitution is **fully decriminalized**, allowing both licensed brothels and independent sex work with minimal restrictions. **Victoria** and **Queensland** have **recently moved to decriminalization**, aiming to treat sex work like any other occupation with protections for workers. In contrast, the **Australian Capital Territory** uses a **legalization model**, where brothels and escort agencies must be licensed, but street-based sex work is largely prohibited. Other regions, such as **Tasmania**, **Western Australia**, and **South Australia**, maintain **stricter controls or partial criminalization**, banning brothels and street solicitation, which can limit safe working conditions for sex workers. Despite these differences, most jurisdictions aim to balance public health, safety, and workers' rights through their regulatory frameworks.

The root causes of prostitution in Australia often relate to socio-economic factors like poverty, unemployment, lack of education, and past trauma or abuse. For many, sex work is a voluntary profession, while for others it may be tied to vulnerabilities such as homelessness or substance dependency. Indigenous and marginalized communities are

---

8   https://www.catwa.org.au/prostitution-laws-in-each-state/

disproportionately represented in the sex industry, highlighting deeper social inequalities.

Societal attitudes toward prostitution in Australia remain mixed but increasingly pragmatic. While stigma and moral concerns persist, there is growing acceptance of sex work as legitimate labor that requires legal protections, health services, and support. Ongoing public debates focus on issues such as human trafficking, safety, and regulation reforms, reflecting the diversity of views and a collective effort to improve conditions for sex workers across the country.

Laws and Penalties[9]

Prostitution in Australia is **regulated primarily at the state and territory level**, resulting in varying rules and enforcement practices. Regulation often focuses on licensing and zoning, especially concerning brothels and street-based sex work. In jurisdictions where brothels are legal or licensed, they must comply with health and safety regulations, including regular inspections and mandatory health checks for workers. Some areas designate specific zones where street prostitution is allowed, while others ban it entirely to manage public order and community concerns.

Sex workers in many states are required to register or obtain licenses, undergo health checks, and adhere to workplace safety standards. These requirements aim to protect both workers and clients, reduce the spread of sexually transmitted infections, and prevent exploitation. Decriminalized areas typically emphasize harm reduction and voluntary compliance rather than punitive measures.

Penalties for prostitution-related offenses vary widely depending on the jurisdiction and the nature of the violation. Common infractions include soliciting in prohibited areas, operating an unlicensed brothel, or involvement in coercion or trafficking. Penalties can range from fines to imprisonment, with harsher sentences applied for offenses involving minors, exploitation, or violence. For example, street solicitation in

---

9   https://en.wikipedia.org/wiki/Prostitution_in_Australia

banned areas often leads to fines or warnings, while running an illegal brothel can result in substantial fines and jail time. Overall, Australian laws seek to balance public health and safety with the protection of sex workers' rights.

Prostitution Practices

Prostitution in Australia involves a variety of practices and forms, with close to 21,000 sex workers across the country as of the most recent data.[10] The industry includes **street-based sex work, brothels, escort services**, and **online sex work**, each regulated differently depending on the state or territory.

Street-based sex work is decriminalized in places like New South Wales and the Northern Territory, allowing workers to operate with fewer legal risks, but it remains largely criminalized in states such as South Australia and Western Australia. **Brothels** are legal and regulated in states like New South Wales and Victoria, where they must comply with local council planning and health regulations. In contrast, brothels are illegal in South Australia and Western Australia. **Escort services** operate legally in some regions, like Queensland and the Australian Capital Territory, where licensing is required, and these services often involve meeting clients at hotels or private residences. The rise of digital platforms has also led to growth in **online sex work**, including webcam and digital content creation, though legal regulations around this form remain less clear and vary by jurisdiction.

Local authorities' attitudes toward prostitution reflect these varied legal frameworks. In decriminalized regions such as New South Wales and the Northern Territory, sex work is treated more as a **legitimate occupation**, with a focus on health and safety for workers. However, in states where prostitution is criminalized or partially criminalized, including South Australia and Western Australia, authorities tend to adopt a more **enforcement-centered approach**, which can create challenges for protecting the safety and rights of sex workers. Overall, the landscape of

10 https://en.wikipedia.org/wiki/Prostitution_statistics_by_country

prostitution in Australia is complex, shaped by differing legal approaches and societal attitudes across states and territories.

Sex Trafficking and Exploitation

Sex trafficking and exploitation are **significant concerns** in Australia, with the Australian Federal Police (AFP) receiving approximately 380 reports of modern slavery in the 2023–24 period. Among these, human trafficking—including entry, exit, and child trafficking—was the most reported form, accounting for about 110 cases. Other prevalent issues included forced marriage, forced labor, sexual exploitation, and domestic servitude.[11]

Certain regions are more vulnerable to sex trafficking due to factors like high demand for sex work, transient populations, and international connections. The Northern Territory, for instance, has been identified as a hotspot for human trafficking activities. In 2024, AFP operations in the Northern Territory and South Australia targeted human trafficking, illicit drugs, and child exploitation, leading to significant arrests and convictions. (Additionally, research identifies that sex trafficking vulnerability is often concentrated in urban centers and **regions with higher migrant populations**. Organized crime groups traffic individuals primarily from Southeast Asian countries, exploiting migratory routes and debt bondage. These victims are typically recruited under deceptive terms and forced into sex work to repay inflated debts.[12]

Demographically, **women** and **girls** are most at risk, particularly those from marginalized backgrounds, including **Indigenous communities**, **migrants**, and **international students**. These groups often face vulnerabilities such as language barriers, lack of legal awareness, and limited access to support services, making them prime targets for traffickers.

---

11 https://www.aihw.gov.au/family-domestic-and-sexual-violence/types-of-violence/modern-slavery

12 https://www.semanticscholar.org/paper/Human-Trafficking-and-Sexual-Servitude%3A-Organised-Langhorn/d319a433472ad853c726820b60b4a1c6a0369944

The Australian government has implemented several measures to combat sex trafficking. In May 2023, the government allocated AUD $24.3 million (about $16 million USD), over four years to the **Support for Trafficked People Program** (**STPP**), aiming to enhance support for victims, including extending the minimum support period to 90 days and providing additional assistance for those with children. Additionally, the government established Australia's first federal **Anti-Slavery Commissioner** to coordinate efforts across agencies and sectors. These initiatives are part of Australia's broader strategy to address modern slavery and human trafficking, focusing on prevention, detection, prosecution, and victim support.[13]

 ## Sex Tourism and Public Health

Sex tourism does exist in Australia, though it is not as widespread or high-profile as in some other countries. Major cities **like Sydney**, **Melbourne**, and **Brisbane** attract visitors who seek commercial sex services, often linked to legalized or regulated prostitution areas. Some regions, particularly tourist hotspots, may have more visible sex work industries catering to both locals and visitors. Sex tourism is generally organized through escort agencies, online platforms, and sometimes street-based solicitation, with advertising primarily happening discreetly via websites or social media to avoid legal issues.

Public health concerns connected to sex tourism include the risk of sexually transmitted infections (STIs), exploitation, and challenges in ensuring safe and consensual sex work. Australian health authorities work to mitigate these risks through regular testing, safe sex campaigns, and support services for sex workers. Because prostitution is regulated in many states, this allows for better health monitoring and reduces risks associated with unregulated sex work. Nonetheless, authorities remain

---

13   https://www.antislaverycommissioner.gov.au/

vigilant about illegal or unregulated sectors where health and safety standards might be lower.

Tips to Avoid Being Solicited

- Stay clear of areas in major cities that are known for legal sex work or adult entertainment, especially at night. Examples include parts of Sydney's Kings Cross or Melbourne's St Kilda.

- Bars, clubs, and late-night venues may attract solicitors. Remain aware of your surroundings and avoid engaging with overly persistent strangers.

- If approached in person or contacted online, politely decline and walk away. Ignoring or disengaging helps avoid unwanted attention.

- Choose well-reviewed hotels or hostels, which are less likely to be located near areas where solicitation is common.

- While Australia is generally casual, drawing less attention through modest dress and non-flirtatious behavior can help minimize unwanted approaches, particularly in areas where solicitation is more prevalent.

Law of the Land True Story[14]

A 43-year-old man from Arncliffe, Sydney, Surya Subekti, has been charged with trafficking a 17-year-old girl from Indonesia for alleged

---

14 https://www.theguardian.com/australia-news/article/2024/jul/23/sydney-man-charged-after-allegedly-trafficking-child-from-indonesia-for-sex-work-ntwnfb

sexual exploitation. According to the Australian Federal Police (AFP), Subekti is the alleged ringleader of a trafficking syndicate that smuggled women into Australia to work in the sex industry. His arrest made in July 2024, followed a 20-month joint investigation by the Department of Home Affairs, and Indonesian authorities—code-named Operation Mirani. Authorities allege that Subekti coordinated with a recruiter in Jakarta to bring victims to Australia under false pretenses. At least 16 women have been identified as potential trafficking victims, with links to over 20 brothels across Sydney and the NSW Central Coast. A second suspect, a 35-year-old Sydney woman, has also been implicated for allegedly helping to fraudulently enroll victims as students to extend their visas and further their exploitation.

Subekti faces a maximum penalty of 25 years in prison. The investigation is ongoing, with further charges expected.

LGBTQ

- Homophobia in Australia
- LGBTQ Legislation
- LGBTQ Tourism and Safety Concerns
- General Questions
- Law of the Land Hypothetical

LGBTQ

Homophobia in Australia

Australia's historical relationship with the LGBTQ+ community has been a complex journey from repression to gradual acceptance. For much of the 20th century, same-sex sexual activity was criminalized across all states and territories, reflecting the British colonial legacy. During this time, LGBTQ+ people faced legal penalties, police raids on their social spaces, and widespread social stigma. Activism emerged in the 1970s, with pride marches and community organizing challenging these oppressive norms.

Over the following decades, Australian governments slowly began to decriminalize same-sex relationships, starting with South Australia in 1975. Despite progress, attitudes and government policies were often inconsistent, and discrimination persisted well into the early 21st century. A **landmark moment** came in **2017**, when **same-sex marriage was legalized** nationally after a highly publicized postal survey.

Today, the general cultural attitude in Australia is **largely progressive, with significant public support for LGBTQ+ rights and equality.** Surveys show that a majority of Australians endorse same-sex marriage and anti-discrimination laws. Acceptance tends to be strongest among younger generations and in urban areas, although conservative views remain prevalent in some rural communities and within certain religious groups.

Religious beliefs have historically played a significant role in shaping attitudes toward LGBTQ+ people in Australia. Various Christian denominations, particularly more conservative factions, have opposed LGBTQ+ rights based on moral or doctrinal grounds. This religious influence has often contributed to social resistance against full acceptance. Additionally, Australia's **traditional "mateship" culture** and emphasis on masculine norms have sometimes fostered homophobic attitudes, particularly among men.

Homophobic attitudes still manifest in everyday life in multiple ways. In workplaces, LGBTQ+ individuals may experience subtle forms of discrimination, exclusion, or harassment, even though legal protections exist. Schools remain a challenging environment for many LGBTQ+ youth, with bullying and social exclusion persisting despite anti-bullying programs and inclusive policies. Family rejection is also reported by many LGBTQ+ people, leading to social isolation and increased mental health struggles.

Violence and discrimination against LGBTQ+ Australians continue to be a concern. A report by the Australian Human Rights Commission in 2020 found that nearly 40 percent of LGBTQ+ people experienced discrimination in the previous year. While physical assaults, verbal abuse, hate crimes, and harassment occur, these incidents are believed to be **underreported**. Transgender and gender-diverse individuals are particularly vulnerable, reporting higher rates of violence and discrimination compared to lesbian, gay, and bisexual people.

Several public and cultural figures in Australia openly advocate for LGBTQ+ rights. Politicians like **former Prime Minister Malcolm Turnbull** supported marriage equality, while celebrities such as **Cate Blanchett** and Olympian **Ian Thorpe** have used their platforms to promote LGBTQ+ visibility and acceptance. Advocacy organizations, including **Australian Marriage Equality** and youth groups like **Minus18**, play key roles in advancing rights and social awareness.

LGBTQ Legislation

Australia has developed a **robust legal framework** supporting LGBTQ+ rights, although the level of support can vary somewhat across states and territories. At the federal level, key laws protect LGBTQ+ individuals and promote equality. The most prominent is the **legalization of same-sex marriage in 2017**, a landmark reform that granted marriage equality nationwide after years of advocacy.

Beyond marriage, federal laws such as the **Sex Discrimination Act 1984** include protections that make discrimination on the basis of sexual orientation, gender identity, and intersex status unlawful in areas like employment, education, and the provision of goods and services. This legislation reflects a supportive stance toward LGBTQ+ rights, aiming to prevent unfair treatment and harassment.

In addition to federal protections, each state and territory has its own anti-discrimination laws that often mirror or expand on federal provisions. These regional laws prohibit discrimination based on sexual orientation and gender identity in various settings, including housing, health care, and public accommodation. For example, New South Wales, Victoria, and the Australian Capital Territory have comprehensive anti-discrimination statutes that explicitly cover LGBTQ+ people and include mechanisms for complaint and redress. Conversely, while no jurisdiction in Australia currently endorses outright discriminatory laws against LGBTQ+ individuals, the effectiveness of protections and levels of support can differ. Some regions, particularly urban centers like Sydney and Melbourne, tend to have stronger and more visible support networks, legal safeguards, and inclusive policies compared to more rural or conservative areas.

There are also ongoing efforts to improve legal recognition and rights for transgender and gender-diverse people, including reforms to simplify the process of changing legal gender markers and banning conversion therapy practices in some jurisdictions. However, challenges remain in certain areas, such as healthcare access for transgender individuals and consistent protections across all states.

Overall, Australian law is **broadly supportive of LGBTQ+ rights**, with **substantial protections against discrimination**. While some variation exists between different parts of the country, there is a clear national trend toward increasing equality and legal recognition for LGBTQ+ individuals.

LGBTQ Tourism and Safety Concerns

LGBTQ tourism in Australia is **well-developed** and forms an important part of the country's broader tourism industry. Major cities like Sydney, Melbourne, and Brisbane are known for their **vibrant LGBTQ scenes**, with **Sydney's annual Mardi Gras parade** being **one of the world's most famous LGBTQ festivals**, drawing visitors from across the globe. These cities offer numerous LGBTQ-friendly venues, events, and accommodations, making them popular and welcoming destinations for LGBTQ travelers.

Tolerance toward LGBTQ individuals generally tends to be higher in metropolitan areas and coastal regions, where cultural diversity and progressive attitudes are more prevalent. In contrast, some rural or remote parts of Australia may be less openly accepting due to more conservative social attitudes and limited community resources. However, even in less urbanized areas, outright hostility is relatively rare, and most LGBTQ visitors report feeling safe.

Public displays of affection between LGBTQ individuals are **widely accepted in major cities**, especially in designated LGBTQ-friendly neighborhoods and at community events. While Australia is generally accepting, LGBTQ visitors might still exercise some caution in public spaces outside metropolitan centers, as conservative attitudes can occasionally result in uncomfortable or unwanted attention.

Regarding safety, Australia is considered **relatively safe for LGBTQ tourists** compared to many countries worldwide. However, incidents of discrimination, verbal harassment, or occasional violence do occur, particularly outside major cities or in less tolerant communities. Local authorities and LGBTQ organizations work actively to promote awareness and ensure the safety of LGBTQ visitors. Resources such as dedicated LGBTQ visitor guides and hotlines are available to assist travelers if needed.

 ## General Questions

1. *Do laws in Australia protect homosexual expressions and conduct?* **Yes.** Australian laws do protect homosexual expressions and conduct. Since the late 20th century, laws across all states and territories have decriminalized consensual same-sex sexual activity. Additionally, various laws protect against discrimination based on sexual orientation and gender identity in areas such as employment, education, and access to services. Legal recognition of same-sex relationships, including marriage equality, was nationally established in 2017. However, the degree of protection and social acceptance can vary regionally and culturally within the country.

2. *Are there any specific local customs, laws, or social norms in Australia that LGBTQ+ visitors should be aware of to ensure their safety and comfort during their stay?* **Yes.** LGBTQ+ travelers to Australia should know that while major cities like Sydney and Melbourne are very welcoming, rural areas may be less tolerant. Public displays of affection are generally accepted in cities but might draw attention elsewhere. Overall, Australia is safe for LGBTQ+ visitors, but it's wise to stay aware of local attitudes, especially in more conservative areas.

 **Law of the Land Hypothetical**

HYPOTHETICAL: *Jordan and Alex, a same-sex couple, want to book a room at a local bed and breakfast just outside Melbourne. The owner seems hesitant and asks if they really mean to stay together in the same room. Can a business owner in Australia legally refuse service to a same-sex couple?*

ANSWER: ***No.*** *Under Australian anti-discrimination laws, businesses cannot refuse service based on a person's sexual orientation. These laws protect LGBTQ+ individuals from discrimination in areas including accommodation, employment, and public services. Jordan and Alex have the right to file a complaint with the relevant state or territory anti-discrimination commission if they face discrimination. Most Australian cities are welcoming to LGBTQ+ visitors, and discrimination by service providers is unlawful.*

SEXUALLY MOTIVATED/ VIOLENT CRIMES

SEXUALLY MOTIVATED/ VIOLENT CRIMES

Overview

Sexually motivated and violent crimes are a growing concern in Australia. In 2023, police recorded 36,318 sexual assault victims—an 11% increase from the year before—marking the highest victimization rate (136 per 100,000 people) since national data collection began in 1993. However, these numbers likely understate the true extent of the problem. Only about 23% of women who experience sexual assault report it to police, according to national surveys.[15]

Several factors contribute to the prevalence of sexual violence in Australia. **Economic stress** plays a significant role; women living in financially unstable households are far more likely to experience sexual assault. Cultural and social norms, especially those rooted in **traditional gender roles** and male dominance, are also contributing factors. These attitudes are particularly entrenched in rural and remote communities, where reporting and support options are limited.

The individuals most affected by sexually motivated crimes in Australia are overwhelmingly women and girls. In 2023, 84% of sexual assault

---

15 https://www.abs.gov.au/statistics/people/crime-and-justice/ recorded-crime-victims/latest-release?utm_source

victims were female, and over a third of these were between the ages of 10 and 17.[16] Young adult women face the highest risk. Women living in rural or remote areas are also disproportionately affected. In these regions, the combination of geographic isolation, limited police presence, fewer victim services, and cultural resistance to speaking out contributes to higher rates of underreported sexual violence. Hospitalization rates for family and domestic violence are 49 times higher in very remote areas compared to major cities.[17]

There are clear **regional disparities in sexual violence rates** across Australia. Queensland, for example, is facing a crisis, with rape and attempted rape reports increasing dramatically over the past 20 years. The Northern Territory also sees disproportionately high levels of violence, with residents nearly twice as likely to report victimization compared to the national average. These higher rates often observed in rural and Indigenous communities where access to support and services may be limited.

Overall, while national awareness has grown, especially following high-profile cases and public protests, sexual violence remains both prevalent and deeply underreported in Australia. Efforts are underway to improve data collection and policy responses, but significant social, economic, and cultural barriers still hinder progress.

Related Legislation

In Australia, sexually motivated offenses are governed by both federal and state or territory laws, with each jurisdiction having its own criminal codes. Key legislation includes the state and territory Crimes Acts or Criminal Codes, specific child protection laws, and federal laws like the Criminal Code Act 1995, which handles offenses such as overseas child sex tourism.

---

16 https://www.abs.gov.au/statistics/people/crime-and-justice/
    recorded-crime-victims/latest-release?utm_source

17 https://www.aihw.gov.au/family-domestic-and-sexual-violence/
    understanding-fdsv/factors-associated-with-fdsv

The range of offenses includes sexual assault (non-consensual penetration), indecent assault (non-consensual sexual touching), **child sexual abuse**, **image-based abuse** (sharing intimate images without consent), and **stalking with sexual intent**. Penalties vary depending on the offense and jurisdiction, but they can be severe—up to life imprisonment for aggravated sexual assault or serious child sexual abuse.

Courts consider factors such as the seriousness of the offense, victim impact, and offender background during sentencing. Some jurisdictions impose mandatory minimum sentences and standard non-parole periods, particularly for child sex crimes. Convicted offenders may also be placed on sex offender registers, subject to ongoing reporting and monitoring requirements.

Consent is central to these cases, with Australian law requiring it to be freely and voluntarily given. There are also mandatory reporting obligations for professionals in cases of suspected child sexual abuse. While laws differ across regions, the national framework emphasizes victim protection, offender accountability, and community safety.

 **General Questions**

1. *Pursuant to law, what is the age of consent for sex in Australia?* The age of consent for sex in Australia is 16 years old in most states and territories, including New South Wales, Victoria, Queensland, Western Australia, the Northern Territory, and the Australian Capital Territory. However, in South Australia and Tasmania, the age of consent is 17.

2. *What are prosecution and conviction rates for sex crimes in Australia?* In Australia, the prosecution and conviction rates for sexual assault cases are notably low. For instance, in New South Wales (NSW), only about 15% of reported sexual assault incidents result in charges being laid, and just 7% lead to a guilty

verdict in court. Nationally, data from the Australian Bureau of Statistics indicates that approximately 77% of sexual assault cases that proceed to court result in a guilty outcome.[18]

The significant attrition of cases occurs primarily during the police investigation phase; for example, 85% of reported incidents in New South Wales do not lead to legal action. Additionally, during court proceedings, about two out of five defendants have all charges withdrawn or dismissed.[19] These statistics highlight the challenges within the Australian criminal justice system regarding the prosecution and conviction of sexual assault cases.

3. *What support services are available to victims of sex crimes?*
In Australia, victims of sex crimes have access to a wide range of support services. The national service 1800RESPECT offers 24/7 confidential counseling, crisis support, and referrals. Additional crisis lines like Lifeline and Kids Helpline provide immediate emotional support. Medical care, including forensic examinations and treatment for injuries or infections, is available through public hospitals and specialized sexual assault response teams. Victims can access free counseling and therapy through state-based sexual assault services such as the Centres Against Sexual Assault (CASAs) in Victoria and similar programs in other states.

Legal assistance is provided through state Legal Aid Commissions, and victims can receive guidance and support through the justice system via Victim Witness Assistance Programs. Financial help is available through state victims' compensation schemes and federal programs like Centrelink's crisis payments. For those in need of housing or relocation due to safety concerns, emergency accommodation services operate in all states.

---

18 https://www.abs.gov.au/media-centre/
media-releases/97-cent-sexual-assault-offenders-are-male

19 https://bocsar.nsw.gov.au/media/2024/mr-attrition-sexual-assaults-BB170.html

There are also specialized services for LGBTQ+ individuals, First Nations people, and male survivors, with organizations such as QLife, 13YARN, and MensLine Australia offering culturally and gender-sensitive support. Most services are free, confidential, and designed to support victims through both immediate crisis and long-term recovery.

 ## Law of the Land Hypothetical

HYPOTHETICAL: *Luca, a 30-year-old tourist from Italy, met an Australian woman, Megan, while visiting Melbourne. After a consensual night together, Megan asked to keep some intimate photos of Luca. Weeks later, after an argument, she posted them online without his consent, tagging him and causing him public embarrassment. Can a tourist press charges for image-based abuse in Australia?*

ANSWER: **Yes.** *Under Victorian law, it's a criminal offense to share intimate images without consent, regardless of the victim's citizenship. Luca is protected like any Australian resident. Megan could face up to two years in prison for distributing the images and more if serious harm is proven. Luca also has the right to seek removal of the images and access victim support services like 1800RESPECT and the eSafety Commissioner.*

 ## Takeaways

- Sexual assaults in Australia increased by 11% in 2023, hitting the highest rate since 1993. However, only about 23% of female victims report assaults, with economic hardship and social norms in rural areas driving both prevalence and underreporting.

- Women make up 84% of sexual assault victims, many aged 10 to 17. Young women and those in rural or Indigenous communities face higher risks due to isolation, limited police presence, and cultural barriers.

- Federal and state laws cover offenses like sexual assault, child abuse, and image-based abuse, with penalties up to life imprisonment. Consent is key, and there are mandatory reporting laws for child abuse.

- Victims can access 24/7 counseling (1800RESPECT), medical care, legal aid, financial help, and specialized support for Indigenous, LGBTQ+, and male survivors to aid both crisis and recovery.

ARRESTED IN AUSTRALIA

CHAPTER 10
ARRESTED IN AUSTRALIA

Overview

When traveling in a foreign country, it's imperative to recognize that you are subject to the legal jurisdiction and regulations of that nation. These laws may significantly differ from those in your home country and might not offer the same legal protections you are accustomed to. It's crucial to bear in mind that penalties for violating foreign laws can be more severe than those for similar offenses in your home country, and ignorance of these laws is not typically accepted as a defense.

The consequences for breaking the law while abroad can be severe and may include expulsion, fines, arrest, or imprisonment. Even unintentional violations can lead to serious legal repercussions. It is essential for travelers to be aware of and adhere to the laws of the host country to avoid legal entanglements and ensure a safe and enjoyable experience.

Specifically, stringent penalties are often enforced for possession, use, or trafficking of illegal drugs in many countries. Convicted offenders can expect severe consequences, including lengthy jail sentences and hefty fines. The legal processes for foreigners in the event of an arrest abroad involve being charged or indicted, prosecuted, potentially convicted and sentenced, and, if applicable, going through an appeals process.

Navigating a foreign legal system can be complex, and individuals arrested abroad must be prepared to comply with the legal procedures of the host country. Seeking legal representation and understanding the local legal nuances are crucial steps for those facing legal issues in a foreign jurisdiction.

Awareness of and adherence to the laws of a foreign country are paramount when traveling. Understanding the potential consequences for legal violations and being prepared to navigate the legal system of the host country are essential aspects of responsible international travel.

Arrest Process

In Australia, common criminal charges include theft, assault, drug offenses, sexual assault, robbery, fraud, and property damage, with serious crimes like murder and drug trafficking carrying heavier penalties. The arrest process begins when police have reasonable grounds to believe a person has committed, is committing, or is about to commit a crime. The arrested individual must be informed that they are under arrest and the reason for it. Police may use reasonable force if necessary. The person has the right to remain silent and to seek legal representation, and they should be clearly informed of these rights, including the right to contact a lawyer. In many places, they also have the right to communicate with someone like a family member or consulate.

Following arrest, the police may detain you for an initial period of up to four hours to conduct investigations or two hours if you are a juvenile or an Aboriginal or Torres Strait Islander. An application can be made to allow an extension of up to a further eight hours. Following this, you must either be charged or released. However, it is important to note that certain periods can be disregarded or constitute 'time outs' for the purposes of this four hours: for example, time waiting for recording facilities, time to allow the accused to communicate with a lawyer or support person, or time for the accused to recover from intoxication.

If you are charged, you will usually be released on bail, with or without conditions. If you are refused bail, or cannot meet the conditions set, you must be brought as soon as practicable before a court where you can apply for bail.

Foreigners have the same legal rights as Australian citizens during this process, but they also have the additional right to contact their embassy or consulate, which police must inform them about. If language barriers exist, interpreters must be provided so the arrested person fully understands their rights and the process. Police are expected to treat foreign nationals with cultural sensitivity throughout.

Getting Legal Assistance

In Australia, everyone who is arrested has the legal right to consult a lawyer and have legal counsel during police questioning and court proceedings. This right applies equally to both citizens and foreign nationals. If you are a foreigner, you also have the right to contact your country's embassy or consulate, which can provide assistance, advice, and help ensure your rights are respected.

If you get arrested in Australia, it's important to remain calm, clearly ask to speak to a lawyer as soon as possible, and exercise your right to remain silent until your lawyer is present. You should also inform the police that you wish to contact your embassy or consulate.

Australia has free or low-cost legal aid organizations available to help those who cannot afford private lawyers. Each state and territory has its own legal aid organizations that offer legal advice, assistance, and representation in criminal and civil matters. These services ensure access to justice regardless of financial status.

Here are some key legal aid organizations in Australia that can assist tourists and other individuals needing legal help:

- **Legal Aid Commissions:** Each state and territory has a Legal Aid Commission offering free or low-cost legal advice and representation.
- **LawAccess NSW:** A government service providing free legal information, referrals, and advice for people in New South Wales, accessible at https://www.lawaccess.nsw.gov.au.
- **Community Legal Centres (CLCs):** These non-profit organizations provide free legal advice and support, especially for vulnerable

groups, including tourists facing legal issues. You can find a local CLC through the national directory at https://www.clcnsw.org.au.

- **National Association of Community Legal Centres:** This body can help locate legal aid and community legal centers across Australia. (https://www.naclc.org.au)

For tourists, these organizations can provide guidance on rights, representation, and support through legal processes, often at no cost or on a sliding scale based on financial need. Additionally, consulates can often help connect tourists with local legal resources.

Bail[20]

Australia has a well-established bail system designed to balance the rights of individuals with community safety and the integrity of the judicial process. Bail allows a person who has been charged with an offense to be released from custody while awaiting their court hearing or trial, usually under specific conditions to ensure they appear in court and do not commit further offenses.

When someone applies for bail, either at the police station or in court, authorities consider **several factors**. These include the **seriousness and nature of the alleged offense**, the **risk that the person might flee** or not appear for court, their **past criminal record**, their **ties to the community** (such as family, employment, or residency), and whether there is a risk they might interfere with witnesses or evidence. Bail can be granted with various conditions such as regular check-ins with police, surrendering a passport to prevent travel, restrictions on movement or contact with certain people, or residing at a particular address.

For visitors or foreign nationals, bail can be more complicated. Since they often lack strong community ties and have the ability to leave the country more easily, courts may view them as a higher flight risk. This can lead to stricter bail conditions, higher bail amounts, or even refusal of bail in some cases. Foreign visitors may also face practical challenges,

20 https://www.courts.qld.gov.au/going-to-court/understanding-bail

such as difficulty finding a surety (someone who pledges to ensure they comply with bail conditions) or meeting financial bail requirements. Additionally, language barriers and unfamiliarity with the legal system can make navigating bail more difficult for tourists.

Bail laws and procedures do **vary somewhat across Australia's states and territories** because each jurisdiction has its own legislation governing bail. While the core principles are similar nationwide—such as assessing flight risk, seriousness of the offense, and risk to the community—the specific rules, processes, and bail conditions can differ.

For example:

- **Queensland** uses the *Bail Act 1980* and has a detailed bail decision framework including "unacceptable risk" tests.
- **New South Wales** operates under the *Bail Act 2013*, with distinct criteria and considerations, such as the "show cause" requirement for certain serious offenses.
- **Victoria** follows the *Bail Act 1977*, with its own guidelines about who decides bail and what conditions can apply.
- **Western Australia** has the *Bail Act 1982* with different procedures for police versus court bail.
- The **Northern Territory**, **Tasmania**, **South Australia**, and the **Australian Capital Territory** each have their own bail laws reflecting local legal priorities.

While the overall purpose of bail—to allow release pending trial with conditions—is consistent, differences exist in how strictly bail is granted, what conditions are common, and which offenses require stricter scrutiny or mandatory refusal of bail.

It's important for visitors arrested in Australia to seek legal advice as soon as possible to understand their rights and options related to bail. Embassies or consulates can often provide guidance or help connect detainees with legal aid services. While the bail system operates uniformly across Australia, visitors should be aware of the additional scrutiny and challenges they may face due to their temporary status in the country.

Complaints Against Police

Australia's police forces are generally viewed as professional and well-organized, but public confidence varies across communities. While many Australians trust the police, some groups—particularly Indigenous Australians, migrants, and young people—report frequent negative interactions, including racial profiling and heavy-handed tactics. These tensions have led to calls for increased oversight and reform in certain jurisdictions.

The most common complaints made against police in Australia involve excessive use of force, racial discrimination, unlawful searches and detentions, verbal abuse, and failure to properly investigate reported crimes. Misconduct during arrests and in police custody is also a recurring concern, particularly in remote and underserved communities.

Filing a complaint against police usually starts by contacting the relevant police department's internal complaints unit, either online, by phone, or in person at a local station. Each state and territory also has an independent watchdog agency responsible for overseeing police behavior, such as the Law Enforcement Conduct Commission in New South Wales, IBAC in Victoria, or the Crime and Corruption Commission in Queensland. These agencies review serious allegations like corruption, assault, or abuse of power. Complaints should include details such as dates, locations, and any available evidence. Anonymous complaints are typically accepted but may be harder to investigate.

There are also several human rights organizations that assist individuals—especially foreign visitors or marginalized groups—who wish to pursue complaints against law enforcement. They include:

Australian Human Rights Commission

Website: https://humanrights.gov.au
Phone: 1300 656 419

Human Rights Law Centre

Website: https://hrlc.org.au

Email: info@hrlc.org.au

Flemington & Kensington Community Legal Centre (Police Accountability Project)

Website: https://www.policeaccountability.org.au

Phone: +61 3 9376 4355

Redfern Legal Centre (NSW-based, focuses on police complaints)

Website: https://rlc.org.au

Phone: +61 2 9698 7277

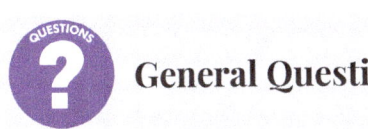 # General Questions

1. *If I am convicted in Australia, how likely am I to be released on bail pending the outcome of my appeal?* If you're convicted in Australia and appeal, you may be granted bail, but it's not automatic. Courts consider the seriousness of the offense, the likelihood of the appeal succeeding, risk of fleeing (especially for tourists), and potential public safety concerns. Foreign nationals often face stricter conditions, like surrendering passports or posting sureties. Bail is more likely if the sentence is short or the appeal raises strong legal issues.

2. *What influences a bail determination?* Bail determinations in Australia are influenced by the seriousness of the offense, risk of the accused fleeing or reoffending, likelihood of appearing in court, the strength of the evidence, the person's criminal history, and any threat to public safety. Personal circumstances, like ties to the community or health issues, can also play a role.

3. *Who is entitled to bail?* In Australia, anyone charged with a criminal offense is generally entitled to apply for bail, but it is not guaranteed. Courts assess each case individually, and for serious offenses like murder or terrorism, the accused must show why detention is not justified—known as a "show cause" or "exceptional circumstances" requirement.

4. *If I am arrested, how soon will I see a judge or magistrate?* If you're arrested in Australia and held in custody, you must be brought before a judge or magistrate "as soon as practicable," usually **within 24 hours**. Delays beyond this are rare and must be justified.

5. *Will I be able to contact my country's embassy in Australia?* **Yes.** If you're arrested in Australia, you have the right to contact your country's embassy or consulate. Police are required to inform foreign nationals of this right and assist in making contact without undue delay.

JAILS VS. PRISONS: CONDITIONS & CULTURE

JAILS VS. PRISONS: CONDITIONS & CULTURE

Overview

Australia's prison system operates on a **state and territory level**, with each jurisdiction managing its own correctional services in addition to a separate federal system for federal offenders. While striving for a balance between punishment and rehabilitation, the system is characterized by a **relatively high incarceration rate** compared to other developed nations. A concerning aspect is the disproportionate representation of Indigenous Australians within the prison population, reflecting broader societal inequities and systemic issues.

In Australia, the terms "jail" and "prison" are often used interchangeably in everyday language, and even by those incarcerated, who frequently refer to their prison as "jail". While historically, **"jail" or "gaol"** (an older spelling) might have indicated short-term detention, like holding cells at a police station, and **"prison"** denoted a place for longer sentences, this distinction has blurred over time. Officially, correctional services prefer the term "correctional centre" or "correctional facility" to describe most prisons, reflecting a focus on rehabilitation alongside punishment. Remand centers, where individuals are held while awaiting trial, are a separate part of the broader system, housing those not yet convicted. While the terms "jail" and "prison" lack a strict legal definition, their use can sometimes reflect the length of sentence served, with "jail" possibly implying shorter durations and "prison" longer ones. However, these distinctions aren't consistently applied across all states and territories, leading to a degree of ambiguity in their everyday use.[21]

Rehabilitation efforts are a key component, with various programs designed to address offending behaviors, provide education and vocational training, and facilitate reintegration into the community. However, the effectiveness of these programs remains a subject of ongoing debate and research. The prison system grapples with a number of challenges including **a growing prison population, concerns about overcrowding and the high costs of incarceration**. Additionally, the effectiveness of current rehabilitation strategies is questioned, and recidivism rates remain high, highlighting the need for more robust throughcare and reintegration support.

Prison types range from **public facilities** to a smaller proportion of **privately operated institutions**, as well as **specialized high-security prisons** for extremely high-risk individuals. Sentencing practices involve judicial discretion within legal boundaries, with the aim of just punishment, deterrence, rehabilitation, denunciation, and community protection. There has also been a trend towards mandatory sentencing laws in recent years, which limit judicial discretion and have sparked varying perspectives. Ultimately, the Australian prison system faces a complex and evolving landscape, necessitating ongoing efforts to address its challenges and enhance its effectiveness.

Prison Conditions and Living Environment

Prison conditions in Australia **vary significantly** depending on the security classification of the facility, the jurisdiction in which it is located, and whether it is publicly or privately operated. Inmates are housed in units based on security risk assessments, which determine whether they are placed in **minimum, medium,** or **maximum-security environments**. These classifications are influenced by the **nature of the offense, criminal history, behavior in custody,** and **risk of escape or harm to others**.

---

21 https://vanessaash.com.au/whats-the-difference-jail-and-prison/

Minimum-security facilities often resemble open campuses with fewer physical barriers, and inmates may have more freedom of movement and opportunities for work. **Medium-security prisons** include more structured routines and restricted movement, while **maximum-security prisons** impose tight controls, limited association with other inmates, and high surveillance. Most prisons consist of cell blocks or dormitory-style housing, with some maximum-security facilities using solitary confinement or segregation for high-risk individuals or disciplinary reasons.

Access to health care in Australian prisons is a mandated responsibility, but the quality and timeliness of services vary. Each state and territory is required to provide prisoners with **medical, dental, and mental health care** equivalent to that available in the community. In reality, many facilities struggle with understaffing, long wait times, and resource limitations. Mental health services, in particular, are frequently under strain, as a significant proportion of inmates enter custody with pre-existing conditions. Some jurisdictions operate specialized forensic mental health units or offer limited psychiatric support within general prisons, but demand often outpaces availability. Chronic illnesses, infectious diseases, and injuries from prison violence also contribute to the burden on health care systems. Indigenous prisoners and those with disabilities face additional barriers in accessing culturally appropriate or tailored care, which can lead to poorer health outcomes during and after incarceration.

Meeting basic needs such as **food, sanitation**, and **hygiene** is a legal obligation for correctional facilities, but the **standard of provision can vary.** Meals are typically prepared onsite and are designed to meet minimum nutritional guidelines, though complaints about food quality and cultural inappropriateness are common. Inmates with specific dietary needs—such as vegetarian, halal, or diabetic diets—can request accommodations, but delays and limited options sometimes lead to dissatisfaction.

Sanitation facilities, including showers and toilets, are generally available, but overcrowding can strain these resources and reduce privacy. Personal hygiene items such as soap, toothpaste, and menstrual products are distributed regularly, though access may be limited in some cases by budget constraints or institutional policies. Temperature control, ventilation, and lighting also affect the overall living environment and vary depending on the age and condition of the facility. While newer prisons tend to be cleaner and better equipped, older institutions often struggle with maintenance issues that negatively impact inmate wellbeing.

Inmate Rights and Legal Protections[22]

In Australia, inmates retain certain legal rights even while serving a prison sentence, although these rights are **subject to limitations** based on security, discipline, and the operational requirements of correctional facilities. Unlike in the United States, Australia does not have a single written constitution that explicitly outlines the rights of prisoners. However, inmates are still protected under common law, state and federal legislation, and international human rights obligations, including the **International Covenant on Civil and Political Rights (ICCPR)**, to which Australia is a signatory. These rights include the right to humane treatment, protection from torture and inhumane punishment, access to health care, and freedom from discrimination. States and territories also have correctional services acts that provide specific guidance on prisoner treatment. For example, the **Corrections Act 1986 (VIC)** and the **Crimes (Administration of Sentences) Act 1999 (NSW)** outline minimum standards for prison management, including requirements for accommodation, safety, and communication with legal representatives.

Prisoners in Australia have the right to access legal resources and to pursue appeals or lodge complaints against their convictions or conditions of confinement. Most correctional facilities have legal libraries or provide limited access to legal materials and support services. Inmates may also request contact with legal aid organizations or private lawyers, and visits for legal consultations are generally permitted without staff monitoring to preserve confidentiality. Appeals against conviction or sentence are heard by state or territory courts, and prisoners can also submit complaints to ombudsman offices or human rights commissions if they believe their treatment violates legal standards. Legal services such

---

22 https://nt.gov.au/law/prisons/prisoners-rights

as **Legal Aid**, **Aboriginal Legal Services**, and **Justice Connect** often assist prisoners with navigating the complex legal system, especially those who are economically or socially disadvantaged.

Despite these protections, issues of abuse and mistreatment within Australian prisons continue to raise serious concerns. Allegations of excessive force by prison officers, misuse of solitary confinement, racial discrimination—particularly against Indigenous inmates—and failures to provide adequate medical or mental health care are recurring themes in media reports and oversight investigations. Legal recourse for inmates who experience abuse exists but is often difficult to pursue. Institutional barriers such as limited access to legal counsel, fear of retaliation, or lack of trust in the complaint process can discourage prisoners from reporting mistreatment. Oversight bodies like the **Inspector of Custodial Services** (in states like Western Australia and New South Wales) and **ombudsman offices** play a critical role in investigating complaints, monitoring conditions, and recommending reforms. However, their powers vary by jurisdiction and are sometimes criticized as insufficiently robust.

 **General Questions**

1. *What is the difference between a jail and prison in Australia?*
   In Australia, jails (called remand centers) hold people awaiting trial or serving short sentences, while prisons house those convicted of serious crimes serving longer sentences (2 years or more). Jails are usually lower security, and prisons can range from minimum to maximum security.

2. *Do jails and prisons offer religious services to inmates?* Yes.
   Both jails and prisons in Australia offer religious services to inmates. Chaplains from various faiths visit regularly to provide spiritual support, lead worship services, and offer counseling.

These services aim to support inmates' mental well-being, rehabilitation, and freedom of religion.

3. *How do prisoners spend their time?* Prisoners in Australia follow a structured daily routine. They often work in prison jobs such as cleaning, kitchen duties, or maintenance. Many also take part in education and vocational training. Rehabilitation programs are common and focus on issues like substance abuse, anger management, and criminal behavior. Inmates have scheduled time for physical exercise and recreation, with access to outdoor yards or gyms. During their free time, prisoners may read, watch TV, or pursue hobbies. The overall aim is to support rehabilitation and reduce reoffending.

4. *How does the prison commissary system work in Australia?* In Australia, the prison commissary system—often called the "buy-up" system—allows inmates to purchase personal items using money from their prison trust account. Family and friends can deposit money into this account, and prisoners may also earn small wages through prison jobs.

Each week, inmates fill out an order form to buy approved items like snacks, toiletries, stationery, and phone credit. Orders are processed and delivered on a set day. The system is strictly regulated, with limits on what and how much can be purchased to maintain security and fairness.

5. *What is prison culture in Australia?* Prison culture in Australia refers to the unwritten rules, behaviors, and social structures that develop among inmates. It often includes strong hierarchies based on factors like the nature of a person's crime, reputation, and time served. Respect and loyalty are important, and breaking social codes can lead to conflict or isolation. Violence and intimidation can occur, especially in higher-security facilities, though efforts are made to reduce this through supervision and rehabilitation. There is also a strong sense of group identity, with inmates forming social circles for support or protection. Some prisoners may join groups based on ethnicity, shared interests, or background. At the same time, many inmates focus on

self-improvement, using education, work, or religious services to cope with prison life. Overall, prison culture can vary by facility, but it plays a major role in how inmates adapt and interact.

HELPING A FRIEND OR RELATIVE IMPRISONED IN AUSTRALIA

HELPING A FRIEND OR RELATIVE IMPRISONED IN AUSTRALIA

Overview

Discovering that a friend or family member has been arrested or imprisoned while traveling in Australia can be incredibly stressful, especially if you're far away and unsure where to turn. The good news is that Australia has a transparent legal and correctional system, and with the right information, you can take practical steps to support your loved one.

The first priority is finding out **where the person is being held**. Each Australian state and territory manages its own correctional system, so your first step is to determine where the arrest occurred. If the arrest was recent, the person may still be in a local police station or temporary holding facility. Otherwise, you can contact the corrections department for that state—such as Corrective Services NSW or Corrections Victoria—to request information. In most cases, they can confirm the location of an inmate if you provide identifying details like their full name and date of birth. Due to strict privacy laws, this is often the only information they can release without the prisoner's consent.

Once you know where the individual is, you can begin coordinating support. If they do not already have legal representation, it's important to **connect with a local lawyer** or contact the **state's Legal Aid Commission**. Legal Aid services can offer free or low-cost legal guidance, especially for individuals facing criminal charges who may not be able to afford private counsel. There are also community-based organizations that offer support to prisoners and their families. Groups such as the Prisoners' Legal Service (in Queensland) can provide information about prisoner rights, family contact, and legal procedures.

Equally important, you should **contact your country's embassy or consulate** in Australia. While consular officers cannot secure a prisoner's release, provide legal advice, or pay legal fees, they can be very helpful in other ways. They may visit the prisoner, ensure that their basic rights are respected, assist with arranging legal counsel, and help the prisoner maintain contact with family. In some cases, they can also help facilitate the transfer of funds or provide a list of English-speaking lawyers.

Maintaining contact with a loved one in prison is possible, though it requires following certain procedures. Most facilities allow inmates to receive letters, make phone calls, and in some cases, participate in video visits. Families usually need to be added to an approved list before contact can be made. Visits must be booked in advance, and strict identification and security rules apply. If you wish to send money to the inmate—for phone credit or to purchase items from the prison store—each state has its own payment system and limits, which are usually outlined on the correctional department's website.

There are a few country-specific tips worth noting. Australia has **strong privacy protections**, so unless the inmate gives written consent, prison staff cannot share personal information about their health, case, or sentence—even with immediate family. Interpretation services are available for non-English speakers, and most legal and government services can arrange interpreters at no cost. Prisoners in Australia also have guaranteed rights to safety, healthcare, and legal representation. If you have serious concerns about the person's treatment, you can contact oversight bodies such as the state Ombudsman or an independent prison inspector.

Above all, try to **stay calm and organized**. Keep a record of names, phone numbers, and case details. Be patient—prison procedures may feel slow, but they are structured and consistent. Your support, even from afar, can make a meaningful difference to someone facing a difficult situation in an unfamiliar country.

Sending Food, Supplies, and Money to an Inmate

In Australia, family and friends **cannot bring or send food** directly to someone in jail or prison. The correctional system across all states and territories has **strict rules that prohibit outside food** from being delivered or brought in during visits. This is mainly due to security, health, and safety concerns. Instead, prisoners buy food and snacks through the **prison canteen or commissary**, which offers a range of items such as instant noodles, biscuits, drinks, and toiletries. The selection varies slightly depending on the facility and state. Prisoners use money from their prison account—funds sent by family and friends or earned through in-prison work programs.

Some correctional systems do allow **care packages on special occasions**, but these are tightly controlled. For example, New South Wales occasionally permits approved "property drop-offs" during designated periods, but these are limited to non-food items like clothing or books and only with prior approval.

If a loved one wants to support a prisoner's food access, the best (and usually only) way is to **transfer money** to their prison account following the rules of the specific facility or state corrections department. Each state has its own process—some allow online payments, others use bank transfers or money orders.

You can send money to someone in an Australian prison, but it has to be done through the **official process set by the state or territory** where they're being held. Each state manages its own correctional system, so the exact method can vary, but the general idea is the same. In **New South Wales**, for example, you can send money using a service called Secure Payment Services or through Australia Post's Post Billpay system. To do that, you need to know the inmate's Master Index Number (MIN) and the name of the facility where they're located. In **Victoria**, the process usually involves using a money order from Australia Post or transferring funds online, depending on the specific prison. You'll need the person's Corrections Reference Number (CRN), their full name, and the name of the prison. In **Queensland**, Secure Payment Services is also used, along with other options like BPAY or sending a cheque or money order, again depending on the individual prison's setup.

No matter the state, there are some common rules. You can't send cash, either by mail or in person. The money must always be sent with the correct prisoner details, like their full name and ID number, and it has to go through approved channels. There's also usually a limit on how much money an inmate can receive or spend in a given week. All transfers are screened by the prison authorities, so if anything seems suspicious—like a large or unusual deposit—it might be flagged or even blocked.

If you're planning to send money, it's always a good idea to check the website of the relevant state's corrections department for the most accurate and up-to-date instructions. Each prison may have slightly different guidelines, but as long as you follow the official process and include the right details, you can help make sure your friend or relative has access to the essentials they need while inside.

Mail, Phone Calls, and Visitation

Inmates in Australia are allowed to receive mail, make phone calls, and have visitors, but everything is regulated under strict rules that can vary a little depending on the state or territory. Still, the basic principles are fairly consistent across the country.

Prisoners can receive letters, and this is often one of the main ways they stay in touch with friends and family. **Mail** is delivered through the regular postal service and goes through a **screening process for safety**. Most facilities have rules about what can and can't be sent—letters are allowed, but things like Polaroids, stickers, or anything glued or stapled are usually banned. If you want to send anything more than a simple letter, like photos or drawings, it's best to check the specific prison's guidelines first.

Phone access is also available, though **prisoners can't receive calls—** they can only make them. Calls are made through a prison-managed phone system, often using pre-approved phone numbers and paid for through the inmate's account. Calls are usually limited in length and are monitored or recorded, unless the call is to a legal representative. Each state has slightly different rules, but generally, prisoners must submit a list of approved contacts, and only those numbers can be called. Some states also allow phone access in languages other than English or through interpreter services, and many prisons have added support for monitored video calls since the COVID-19 pandemic.

When it comes to visits, inmates are **generally allowed to receive visits from family and approved friends**, but how often and how long depends on the prison. You usually need to book your visit in advance and be on the inmate's approved visitor list. Identification is required when you arrive, and you'll have to pass through security checks. Visits may be contact or non-contact, depending on the prison's classification of the inmate or any restrictions currently in place.

There are a few important things to know before visiting. You can't bring in personal items like bags, phones, or food, and dress codes are enforced—clothing that's too revealing, torn, or resembles a uniform might not be allowed. You also can't give anything directly to the inmate. Some facilities have lockers where you can store your belongings, and most will have waiting areas or reception desks where you check in before being escorted to the visit area. Rules are strict, but visits are encouraged as they're seen as important for rehabilitation and maintaining family ties.

Prison Scams

Although not extremely common, there have been scams in Australia that target the families of inmates. When they do happen, they usually involve **fake legal help**, **fraudulent payment services**, or **impersonators** claiming to be officials. These scams can be emotionally manipulative and are often aimed at people who are desperate to help their loved ones.

One type of scam involves someone posing as a lawyer or prison official who contacts the family, claiming that money is urgently needed for bail, legal fees, or early release processing. They might ask for payment through untraceable means like gift cards, cryptocurrency, or money transfer apps. This is a red flag—real legal professionals or prison staff will never demand money this way or promise quick release for a fee.

Another variation targets families sending money to inmates. Some scammers set up fake websites or social media pages that claim to process payments to prison accounts. If you use these unofficial channels, the money disappears and never reaches the inmate. Always use the official payment services listed on the relevant state correctional services website—those are the only ones authorized to process inmate funds. There have also been cases of people pretending to be fellow inmates or friends of the incarcerated person, reaching out to family members with a story about needing money for food, court costs, or protection inside prison. These scams often rely on emotional manipulation and a sense of urgency.

To protect yourself, **don't send money through unverified websites, don't give out personal or financial information** over the phone or through email unless you're absolutely sure of the identity of the person contacting you, and **always verify legal representation** directly through official directories or state legal aid services. If something feels off—like pressure to act fast or secrecy about the situation—it's worth stopping and checking before you do anything.

If you believe you've been targeted or scammed, **report it to the Australian Cyber Security Centre (https://www.cyber.gov.au/) or Scamwatch (https://www.scamwatch.gov.au/).** If money has already been transferred, contact your bank or payment provider immediately to see if the transaction can be reversed. Keeping a clear record of communication, verifying identities, and using only official channels is the best way to avoid falling victim to these scams.

Upon Release

When a foreign national is released from prison or jail in Australia, there are usually **specific legal and immigration consequences** they'll need to deal with—sometimes immediately upon release. In most cases, **non-citizens who serve a prison sentence of 12 months or more** are referred to the **Department of Home Affairs**, which can review their visa status. Under Australian immigration law, a non-citizen's visa can be **cancelled** on "character grounds" if they've been convicted of a serious crime. This means that even if they entered Australia legally, they may not be allowed to stay after release.

If their visa is cancelled, the person is typically transferred directly from prison to an **immigration detention center**, where they may remain while their case is reviewed or while arrangements are made for deportation. In some situations, a former prisoner may appeal the cancellation, but they must do so quickly—often within 9 days of receiving notice.

Even if the person is not deported, they may still face **conditions or reporting obligations** after release, especially if they are on parole. These can include regular check-ins with a parole officer, restrictions on travel, mandatory participation in rehabilitation programs, or curfews. Parole is usually granted with conditions tailored to the case and is strictly monitored. Violating these terms can result in being returned to custody.

For **minor offenses** or **short-term sentences**, some foreign nationals are **released without additional immigration action**. However, if the person was on a temporary visa—like a student or tourist visa—that visa may already have expired by the time of release, in which case they'd need to apply for a bridging visa or prepare to leave the country.

It's strongly recommended that foreign nationals released from custody seek legal advice or speak with immigration services immediately, as the intersection between criminal and immigration law in Australia can be complex and moves quickly. Legal aid may be available, depending on the state and the person's financial situation.

THE ADMINISTRATION OF JUSTICE

CHAPTER 13

THE ADMINISTRATION OF JUSTICE

Australia's Legal System[23]

Australia's legal system is a **common law system**, based on the British model, and shaped by both **statute (legislation)** and **case law (court decisions)**. It operates as a **federal system**, meaning power is divided between the **federal government** and the **six states and two territories**, each of which has its own set of laws, courts, and law enforcement agencies.

The **Australian Constitution**, which came into effect in 1901, outlines the structure of government and the division of powers. The federal government handles national issues like immigration, defense, and foreign affairs, while states and territories deal with matters like policing, education, health, and local justice systems.

Australia has **three levels of courts**: **lower courts** (like Magistrates' Courts), **intermediate courts** (District or County Courts), and **superior courts** (Supreme Courts and the High Court of Australia). Most criminal and civil matters begin in the lower courts. Serious cases, including major criminal trials, may be heard in the higher courts. The **High Court** is the country's top court—it interprets the Constitution, hears appeals, and can overturn decisions from lower courts.

---

23 https://en.wikipedia.org/wiki/Australian_legal_system

The legal system is built on the principle of the **rule of law**, meaning no one is above the law, and laws must be applied fairly. Judges are independent from government, and defendants have the right to a fair trial, legal representation, and the presumption of innocence.

Lawyers in Australia are either **barristers**, who specialize in courtroom advocacy and legal opinions, or **solicitors**, who usually handle legal advice, paperwork, and direct client work. In many areas, the roles can overlap.

Australia's legal system also includes safeguards for **human rights**, though it doesn't have a national bill of rights. Some protections exist through state charters (like in Victoria and the Australian Capital Territory), international treaties, and common law principles.

The three major challenges facing the Australian judicial system are equitable access to justice, Indigenous justice, and the handling of mental health within the legal system. First, **access to justice is uneven**, with disadvantaged groups often unable to afford legal representation or navigate complex court procedures, highlighting the need for clearer, more inclusive processes. Second, **Indigenous Australians remain significantly over-represented** in the criminal justice system, reflecting historical injustices, a lack of trust in legal institutions, and a pressing need for culturally appropriate legal services. Third, the **system struggles to adequately address the needs of individuals with mental health conditions**, who often face prolonged detention or inadequate support due to limited integration between mental health services and the legal process. These challenges, compounded by limited resources and an evolving social landscape, demand coordinated reform to ensure a more just and inclusive system.

 **General Questions**

1. *Do the courts treat first-time offenders and tourists with more leniency?* **Yes.** Australian courts do tend to treat tourists and first-time offenders more leniently, especially when the offense is minor and non-violent. Judges often take into account a person's clean record, genuine remorse, cooperation with authorities, and unfamiliarity with local laws. Tourists, in particular, may benefit from the understanding that they are less likely to reoffend in Australia due to the temporary nature of their stay. For first-time offenders, the courts generally focus more on rehabilitation and deterrence than punishment, and penalties might include fines, community service, or good behavior bonds rather than imprisonment. Some states offer diversion programs or legal provisions. However, leniency is not guaranteed. If the offense is serious, involves violence, or has significant consequences, the courts can and do impose strict penalties, regardless of a person's tourist status or lack of prior convictions. Ultimately, while there is a tendency toward compassion and discretion, each case is assessed individually based on the severity of the offense and the broader public interest.

2. *If I am charged with a crime, which court is likely to hear my case?* If you're charged with a crime in Australia, the court that hears your case depends on the seriousness of the offense. Most minor or summary offenses—like petty theft, public intoxication, or minor drug possession—are handled in the Magistrates' Court (or Local Court in some states). More serious indictable offenses, such as assault or burglary, may start in the Magistrates' Court but are usually sent to a higher court, like the District Court (or County Court in Victoria). The Supreme Court handles the most serious crimes, such as murder. If you're a tourist or first-time offender charged with a minor offense, your case will almost certainly be heard in the Magistrates' Court.

3. *What is the standard of proof in a criminal case in Australia?*
In a criminal case in Australia, the standard of proof is "beyond a reasonable doubt." This means the prosecution must prove the accused's guilt to such a high level that there would be no reasonable doubt in the mind of a fair-minded person. It is a very strict standard, designed to protect individuals from being wrongly convicted. If there is any reasonable doubt about the accused's guilt, the jury or judge must return a verdict of not guilty. This standard applies in all criminal courts across Australia, from the Magistrates' Court to the Supreme Court.

 **Law of the Land Hypothetical**

HYPOTHETICAL: *Amelia, a 24-year-old tourist from Canada, is driving through rural Victoria when she sees a wombat by the roadside. Believing it to be injured or abandoned, she picks it up, films a video with it, and posts it online. A local wildlife group reports her for interfering with a protected species. She is charged under Victoria's Wildlife Act 1975. How is the Australian legal system likely to handle a tourist's first-time wildlife offense?*

ANSWER: *Amelia's case would be heard in a Magistrates' Court, which handles minor (summary) offenses. As a first-time offender and tourist, she would likely receive lenient treatment, especially since she showed remorse and had no intent to harm. The court might impose a small fine, a good behavior bond, or offer a diversion program to avoid conviction. These outcomes reflect the system's focus on fairness, rehabilitation, and public interest—particularly for minor, non-violent offenses.*

 **Takeaways**

- Australia's legal system is a federal common law system based on British law, combining legislation and court decisions, with powers divided between federal and state/territory governments.

- Minor cases usually start in Magistrates' Courts, more serious matters go to District or Supreme Courts, and the High Court is the ultimate appellate court and constitutional interpreter.

- Everyone is equal before the law, judges are independent, and accused persons have rights like having a fair trial and the presumption of innocence.

- First-time offenders and tourists often receive leniency for minor, non-violent offenses, with courts focusing on rehabilitation rather than harsh punishment.

- The system faces major challenges including access to justice for disadvantaged groups, over-representation of Indigenous Australians in courts, and addressing mental health issues within the legal framework.

CRIME VICTIM ASSISTANCE

CRIME VICTIM ASSISTANCE

Overview

In Australia, victims of crime have access to a range of resources designed to provide support, protection, and assistance during and after their experience. These resources come from both government agencies and non-government organizations (NGOs), offering help that includes counseling, legal aid, financial assistance, and safety planning.

Government support for crime victims is provided primarily through **state and territory-based Victim Support Services**. These agencies offer free, confidential services such as counseling, information about the justice process, help with victim impact statements, and referrals to other agencies. They also administer financial assistance programs to help cover expenses related to the crime, such as medical costs or lost income, under schemes like the **Victims of Crime Assistance Tribunal** (**VOCAT**) in Victoria or the **Victims Compensation Tribunal** in New South Wales. Police services often have dedicated victim liaison officers who assist victims throughout investigations. Nationally, the Australian Government funds programs that support victims of family violence, sexual assault, and human trafficking, with services including crisis accommodation and legal aid.

Non-government organizations also play a vital role in supporting crime victims. These include specialist counseling services, shelters, and advocacy groups. For example, organizations like **1800RESPECT** provide a national sexual assault and domestic violence counseling helpline accessible 24/7. Groups such as the **Women's Legal Service Australia** offer legal advice and support for victims of domestic violence. Other NGOs, like **Victim Support Australia**, help coordinate local services and campaigns to raise awareness about victims' rights. Many community organizations provide culturally sensitive and language-specific support, especially for Indigenous Australians and migrants.

Emergency contacts in Australia are straightforward and widely promoted to ensure quick access to help. In life-threatening or urgent situations, dialing **000** connects callers to **police, ambulance,** or **fire services.** For non-emergency police assistance, each state and territory has specific contact numbers. For urgent counseling or crisis intervention related to domestic violence or sexual assault, the national 24-hour helpline **1800RESPECT (1800 737 732)** is available. Additionally, **Lifeline (13 11 14)** offers 24/7 telephone counseling for people experiencing emotional distress or suicidal thoughts.

What to Do If You Are the Victim of a Crime

If you are the victim of a crime in Australia, there are several important steps you should take to ensure your safety, protect your rights, and get the help you need. First and foremost, if you are in immediate danger or need urgent medical assistance, call **000** to reach **emergency services.** Your safety is the highest priority.

Once you are safe, try to **preserve any evidence** related to the crime. Avoid cleaning up the scene, touching objects, or disturbing anything that could be important for an investigation. If you can, write down or record details about what happened, including descriptions of the offender, any witnesses, and the time and place of the incident.

It is important to **report the crime to the police** as soon as possible. You can visit your local police station, call the non-emergency police number in your state or territory, or, if it's an emergency, use **000.** When reporting, provide as much detail as you can. The police will document your statement and begin an investigation. You can ask for the support of a victim liaison officer, who can guide you through the process and keep you informed about the progress of your case.

Seek medical attention even if you don't have visible injuries. A healthcare professional can check for hidden injuries, provide treatment, and document evidence, especially important in cases of assault or sexual violence. Do not hesitate to access support services. Contact your local Victim Support Service or a relevant NGO, such as **1800RESPECT** for domestic or sexual violence, for counseling, legal advice, or assistance with compensation claims. These organizations can provide emotional support and help you understand your rights in the criminal justice system.

Common Tourist Scams in Australia

Tourists in Australia can unfortunately be targeted by a variety of scams designed to exploit their unfamiliarity with the local environment, systems, and regulations. Some common scams include **fake accommodation listings**, where travelers book lodgings online that don't exist or are vastly different from advertised; **rental scams** where scammers pose as landlords and ask for deposits before disappearing; and **taxi or rideshare scams** involving overcharging or taking longer routes.

Another frequent scam targets tourists through **bogus tour operators** offering fake or substandard tours and activities, sometimes disappearing with payments before providing any service. **Pickpocketing** and **distraction scams** are also common in crowded tourist spots, where thieves use tricks like asking for directions or dropping items to divert attention and steal wallets or phones.

Phone and internet scams are increasingly prevalent, including fake calls or messages pretending to be from government agencies, immigration authorities, or local police, demanding payments for fines, visas, or legal troubles. Tourists may also encounter scams involving **counterfeit goods** sold as authentic souvenirs, or street vendors pressuring visitors to buy overpriced items. Finally, scams related to **currency exchange** or **credit card fraud** can occur, such as dishonest money changers offering poor rates or tampered card readers at ATMs or shops.

To avoid falling victim, tourists are advised to verify bookings through official websites, use licensed taxi or ride-share services, be cautious with unsolicited calls or messages, only exchange money at authorized places, and keep belongings secure in public areas. **If you suspect a scam, report it to local police or consumer protection agencies promptly.**

Consular Assistance

If you find yourself the victim of a crime while in Australia, your embassy or consulate can provide important support, although their role has some limits. Primarily, they act as a **liaison between you and the local authorities**, helping you navigate the legal and bureaucratic processes that can be confusing in a foreign country.

Your embassy or consulate can assist by providing a list of local lawyers who speak your language and have experience dealing with cases involving foreign nationals. While they cannot represent you legally or intervene in legal proceedings, they can help you find qualified legal advice or interpreters if needed. They may also help you understand your rights under Australian law and the steps you should take following the crime.

If you have lost your passport or important identification documents due to the crime, your embassy or consulate can issue emergency travel documents to help you continue your journey or return home. They can also assist in contacting your family or friends to inform them of your situation. In cases where you are detained or arrested, consular officials have the right to visit you in detention, ensure you are being treated fairly according to Australian law, and provide a list of local attorneys. However, they cannot get you out of jail or interfere in court decisions.

Additionally, embassies often provide information on local victim support services, medical facilities, and counseling resources that can help you recover physically and emotionally. Some embassies may also offer limited financial assistance or advice on how to access funds if you are stranded or in urgent need.

Overall, while embassies and consulates cannot solve legal matters directly, they serve as a critical support system, helping you navigate the aftermath of being a crime victim in a foreign country and connecting you with the resources you need.

? General Questions

1. *If I am a victim of a crime, can I legally be compensated?*
   Yes. Even as a visitor in Australia, you may be eligible for victim compensation under state or territory schemes. While eligibility can vary, many jurisdictions allow non-residents to apply if they were harmed by a crime in Australia, reported it promptly, and meet other criteria. However, some programs might prioritize residents or have additional requirements for visitors. It's important to contact the local Victim Support Service or Compensation Authority where the crime occurred to understand your specific eligibility and how to apply.

2. *If a family member falls victim to homicide, can I bring the body back to my home country?* **Yes**. If a family member is a homicide victim in Australia, you can arrange to bring their body home. This involves working with local police, the coroner, funeral services, and your country's embassy or consulate to get the necessary documents. The process can take time due to investigations, and costs can be high, but embassies may offer guidance and limited assistance. Close communication with authorities is important to ensure everything is done legally and respectfully.

3. *What protections are in place to ensure the safety and confidentiality of crime victims during legal proceedings?* In Australia, there are strong protections to ensure the safety and confidentiality of crime victims during legal proceedings. Courts can issue special measures such as giving evidence via video link or behind screens to prevent direct contact with the accused.

Victims' identities are often kept confidential, and media reporting may be restricted to protect their privacy.

Victim support officers and legal representatives help victims understand the process and provide emotional support. Laws also prohibit harassment or intimidation of victims related to their involvement in the case.

POLICE

POLICE

Overview

Australia's police force operates under a federal system, meaning law enforcement responsibilities are divided between the **national** and state or territory governments. There is no municipal or city-level police as seen in some other countries. Instead, policing is handled either at the federal level or by each of the six states and two self-governing territories.

At the **federal level,** the **Australian Federal Police**, or **AFP**, is responsible for enforcing national laws, managing counter-terrorism operations, handling cybercrime and organized crime, and providing policing services to external territories like Christmas Island. The AFP also plays an international role, working in global crime investigations and peacekeeping missions. Within the Australian Capital Territory (ACT), the AFP provides local policing services under a contract with the ACT government, effectively functioning as the territory's police force.

Each **state** and **territory** also has its own **police force**, such as the **New South Wales Police Force**, **Victoria Police**, and **Queensland Police Service.** These forces are responsible for day-to-day law enforcement, public safety, community policing, traffic control, and emergency response within their jurisdictions. Even in major cities like Sydney, Melbourne, and Brisbane, local policing is managed by the state police force, not a city department.

In terms of size, the total number of police employees across Australia is estimated to **be around 80,000,** with approximately 66,000 of those being sworn officers.[24] Victoria Police and New South Wales Police are the two largest forces, each employing tens of thousands of personnel. The Australian Federal Police, while smaller in comparison, still maintains a workforce of about **7,000 people,** including both officers and civilian staff.[25] Other states and territories operate smaller forces appropriate to their population size and geographic needs.

Whether the police force is adequately staffed depends on the region. Urban areas typically have better coverage and response times, but rural and remote areas, particularly in the Northern Territory, Western Australia, and parts of Queensland, often experience **significant shortages.** Recruitment and retention can be challenging in these areas due to isolation, harsh working conditions, and limited community infrastructure. Some forces, like those in Victoria and New South Wales, have undertaken major recruitment campaigns to address increasing workloads and rising attrition rates. These efforts aim to bring in new officers while addressing gaps in specialized areas like cybercrime, mental health crisis response, and family violence.

While Australia's overall police-to-population ratio compares well internationally, several police unions and oversight bodies have expressed concern that certain departments are overstretched, particularly when responding to complex social issues that extend beyond traditional crime. Reports have also emphasized the need for more investment in training, technology, and support services to keep up with the evolving demands of modern policing.

---

24 https://www.pc.gov.au/ongoing/report-on-government-services/2025/justice/police-services

25 https://www.transparency.gov.au/publications/attorney-general-s/australian-federal-police/australian-federal-police-annual-report-2023-24/management-and-accountability/our-people

Police Response

Both federal and state/territory police have their own set of responsibilities. The **AFP** operates at the national level and is **responsible for enforcing federal laws.** Its duties include handling complex crimes such as **terrorism, drug trafficking, human trafficking, cybercrime,** and **child exploitation** that often cross state or international borders. The AFP also provides protection services for national political leaders, embassies, and airports, and manages policing for Australia's external territories. In the Australian Capital Territory, the AFP also acts as the local police under a contractual agreement with the ACT government.

State and territory police forces, on the other hand, are responsible for **day-to-day law enforcement** within their respective jurisdictions. These include the New South Wales Police Force, Victoria Police, Queensland Police Service, and their counterparts in other states and territories. Their duties range from **responding to emergency calls** and conducting investigations into local crimes such as **theft, assault,** and **vandalism,** to **managing traffic enforcement, crowd control,** and **missing persons cases.** They also play a key role in **preventing domestic violence** and working with local communities on **crime prevention** and **safety programs.** In regional and remote areas, they often serve as the main or only government service available. Despite the division of responsibilities, there is often close cooperation between the AFP and state police through **joint task forces,** particularly in tackling organized crime, terrorism, and other cross-jurisdictional threats.

The **biggest challenges** facing the police forces in Australia today are both operational and social. **Staffing shortages** are a growing issue, particularly in remote and rural communities, where it is often difficult to recruit and retain officers. These areas frequently report long response times and high stress among limited personnel. Even in more populated regions, police forces are struggling to maintain adequate staffing as retirements increase and the demands of the job grow more complex.

The rise in cybercrime and online exploitation has introduced a new layer of difficulty, requiring **specialized skills and resources** that are often in short supply. While agencies like the AFP are building their capabilities in digital investigation, the pace of technological change often outstrips their ability to keep up.

Mental health is another significant pressure point. Police are increasingly called upon to respond to mental health crises in the community, situations that often require more expertise than officers are trained for. This not only places additional strain on police but also highlights a broader issue with under-resourced mental health services in the country.

Police and Community Relations

The overall reputation of the police in Australia is **generally positive**, but it is nuanced and shaped by a mix of public trust, community engagement, and controversy. Most Australians view their police forces as professional and effective, particularly when it comes to responding quickly to emergencies, preventing crime, and maintaining order in cities and suburbs. National surveys consistently show that a majority of people express confidence in the police, especially when it comes to local policing.[26] This confidence is often strongest in middle-class and urban communities, where people are more likely to see police as approachable and responsive.

However, the relationship between police and certain communities—especially Indigenous Australians and some migrant groups—is more complex and often strained. Indigenous Australians have long-standing concerns about **over-policing**, **racial profiling**, and **excessive use of force**. These concerns are not new; they stem from decades of historical injustice, high rates of Indigenous incarceration, and several high-profile deaths in custody. While police forces have made efforts to improve relationships with Indigenous communities—through liaison programs,

---

26 https://www.abs.gov.au/statistics/measuring-what-matters/
     measuring-what-matters-themes-and-indicators/cohesive/
     trust-key-institutions

cultural awareness training, and community partnerships—many Indigenous people remain distrustful of law enforcement institutions.[27]

Younger Australians, especially those from multicultural or low-income backgrounds, may also view police with skepticism, particularly in areas where **stop-and-search tactics** or **heavy-handed crowd control** are common. There have been public protests and media scrutiny in recent years over specific incidents involving racial profiling or excessive force, which have sparked broader conversations about police accountability and reform.

That said, many police forces across the country actively invest in community outreach, neighborhood policing, and school-based programs to build trust. Officers often participate in local events, visit schools, and work with social service agencies to address issues like youth crime, domestic violence, and mental health crises. These initiatives are generally well-received and help humanize the police in the eyes of the public.

Social media has also become a tool for building community relationships. Police departments regularly use platforms like Facebook and Twitter to share updates, issue warnings, and even post light-hearted content, which has improved their visibility and relatability, especially among younger audiences.

In summary, while Australian police enjoy a relatively high level of public trust overall, this trust is not universal. It varies significantly depending on geography, ethnicity, and past experiences with law enforcement. For many Australians, the police are a dependable and helpful institution. For others, especially those in historically marginalized communities, the relationship is marked by caution, criticism, and calls for reform. The ongoing challenge for police leadership is to continue building bridges where trust has been lost, while maintaining the confidence of the broader public.

---

27 https://www.theguardian.com/australia-news/2023/jul/31/nsw-po-lice-use-force-against-indigenous-australians-at-drastically-dispropor-tionate-levels-data-shows

Police Use of Force

Police use of force is a continuing issue in Australia, drawing both national and international scrutiny, especially in cases involving Indigenous Australians and people with disabilities or mental health challenges. While most officers perform their duties professionally, there have been **repeated incidents** where the use of force appears excessive or poorly managed, raising questions about training, accountability, and systemic bias.

One particularly troubling case occurred in May 2025 in Alice Springs. A 24-year-old Warlpiri man with a known disability died after being restrained by police at a local supermarket. Witnesses claimed the officers ignored warnings about his condition and used aggressive force, including kneeling on his neck. He lost consciousness and later died in hospital. Despite public outcry and calls from the man's family for an independent investigation, Northern Territory Police refused, saying their internal Major Crime Division would lead the inquiry. The incident reignited long-standing concerns about how law enforcement engages with Aboriginal communities, particularly in the Northern Territory, where Indigenous people are significantly overrepresented in arrest and custody statistics.[28]

Such cases are not isolated. They reflect broader concerns about police culture in Australia, especially when dealing with vulnerable populations. Advocacy groups, legal experts, and human rights organizations have called for stronger oversight, body-worn camera mandates, and more rigorous de-escalation training. While reforms are slowly being introduced in some jurisdictions, incidents of excessive force continue to expose gaps in accountability and deepen community mistrust.

---

28 https://www.theguardian.com/australia-news/2025/may/30/family-of-warlpiri-man-who-died-after-being-restrained-by-police-in-supermarket-demand-independent-inquiry-ntwnfb?utm_source

 ## Law of the Land True Story[29]

In 2024, yet another disturbing incident involving an Australian Capital Territory (ACT) police officer came to light, highlighting serious concerns about the treatment of Indigenous youth in custody. During the intake process at a Watch House, the officer was recorded making deeply inappropriate remarks to a 17-year-old Indigenous boy. The officer taunted the teenager by asking, "Are you thinking of necking yourself?"—a colloquial and insensitive reference to suicide. When the boy denied having suicidal thoughts, the officer retorted, "You wouldn't have the guts to do it anyway." Further exacerbating the situation, the officer mocked the boy for being in foster care and lacking parental support. Other officers present reportedly smirked but failed to intervene.

The incident, revealed during an ACT Supreme Court hearing, sparked widespread condemnation. ACT Chief Police Officer labeled the behavior as "unacceptable" and confirmed that the matter was under investigation by the Australian Federal Police's Professional Standards unit. Indigenous advocates and community leaders criticized the remarks as reflective of systemic racism and neglect towards Aboriginal youth.

---

29 https://www.news.com.au/national/nsw-act/courts-law/act-cop-accused-of-horrific-comments-to-17yearold-at-watch-house/news-story/)

CHAPTER 16

HOW TO GET LEGAL
HELP IN AUSTRALIA

- Available Resources
- Legal Aid
- Foreign Embassies in Australia

HOW TO GET LEGAL HELP IN AUSTRALIA

Available Resources

If a tourist is arrested in Australia, finding reliable legal representation is essential and should begin as soon as possible. The first step is to ask the police to contact a **duty lawyer**. A duty lawyer is a lawyer present at court to provide free legal advice and representation to individuals who are unrepresented, particularly in urgent matters. They assist people, especially those from vulnerable backgrounds, by explaining court processes, advising on legal options, and representing them in initial appearances and bail applications. Essentially, duty lawyers are crucial for ensuring access to justice for those who cannot afford a private lawyer, acting as a first point of contact with the legal system and facilitating smoother court operations.

Tourists should also reach out to their country's **embassy or consulate**, which, while not providing legal representation, can offer a list of trusted local lawyers and explain the basics of the legal process. Yet another option is to search the official website of the relevant state's **Law Society or Bar Association**, such as the Law Society of New South Wales or the Law Institute of Victoria, which maintain directories of qualified, licensed lawyers searchable by specialty or location. **Independent legal referral services**, like the Australian Lawyers Alliance or Community Legal Centres, can also help connect tourists to lawyers experienced in handling criminal matters involving foreigners. Once a lawyer is located, it's important to confirm their credentials and ask questions about their experience, fees, and availability to ensure they are a good fit for the case.

Legal Aid[30]

Legal Aid is a system designed to assist those who cannot afford legal representation in Australia. While it primarily focuses on residents and citizens, there may be **some limited exceptions** for specific circumstances, especially if they are faced with urgent or serious legal issues, such as detention or criminal charges. To determine specific eligibility and services, individuals need to contact the **Legal Aid commission** in the relevant state or territory, all of which operate under similar guidelines but may have slight procedural differences. Eligibility is generally determined by three main factors: the type of case, the individual's financial means, and whether the case has legal merit.

Legal aid is primarily available for serious matters such as criminal charges, immigration and asylum issues, family law disputes (particularly involving children or domestic violence), child protection proceedings, mental health matters, and civil cases involving human rights. Foreign nationals who find themselves in such situations—whether they are tourists, temporary visa holders, or undocumented individuals—may qualify for assistance, provided they cannot afford a lawyer and their case falls within one of these approved categories. However, routine civil matters such as commercial disputes, debt collection, or most personal injury claims are not typically covered.

To qualify, a foreign visitor must pass a **means test**, which assesses their income, assets, and financial dependence on others. Even temporary or undocumented visitors may pass this test if they are in financial hardship. The Legal Aid Commission also conducts a **merit test** to ensure the case has a reasonable chance of success and represents an appropriate use of public resources.

---

30 https://www.probonocentre.org.au/legal-help/legal-aid

The application process begins by contacting the Legal Aid Commission in the relevant state or territory—such as Legal Aid NSW, Victoria Legal Aid, or Legal Aid Queensland—either online, over the phone, or in person. Applicants must provide personal identification, including visa status if available, financial documents, and a brief description of the legal issue. If both the means and merit tests are satisfied, legal aid may be granted, and the individual may either be assigned a legal aid lawyer or receive funding to use a private lawyer.

Once approved, legal aid can **cover a range of services** including legal advice, court representation, assistance with legal documents, and interpreters where necessary—especially in immigration or family law matters. While legal aid covers many essential legal services, it does not pay for personal expenses such as travel or accommodation, and does not generally assist with minor civil matters.

Beyond that, there are several legal organizations in Australia that provide free or low-cost legal advice to foreign visitors, even if they are not eligible for government-funded Legal Aid. One of the most accessible options is the network of **Community Legal Centres** (**https://clcs. org.au/**).These are independent, non-profit organizations that operate across Australia and offer free legal advice and assistance to people experiencing hardship or disadvantage, regardless of their citizenship or visa status. Foreign visitors can usually access help through walk-in clinics, phone consultations, or online appointments. Many CLCs specialize in areas like immigration law, housing and tenancy issues, employment disputes, domestic violence, and consumer rights. While they often cannot offer full legal representation, they do provide vital information, draft letters or forms, and sometimes offer advocacy.

Refugee Legal, based in Victoria, also provides expert legal support in immigration and asylum law (**https://refugeelegal.org.au/**). Although it is known for serving refugees and asylum seekers, it offers telephone advice to anyone in Australia needing help with protection visas, detention issues, or related legal matters. This makes it a useful service for foreign visitors facing urgent immigration concerns. Similarly, the **Asylum Seeker Resource Centre** (**ASRC**), headquartered in Melbourne, offers legal services focused on visa applications, appeals, and interventions (**https://asrc.org.au/**). It supports people with little or no income and unstable visa status and provides free legal clinics and advocacy on complex immigration cases.

Justice Connect (https://answers.justiceconnect.org.au/) is another nationwide resource that helps people who do not qualify for Legal Aid but still cannot afford a lawyer. Through its various programs, it links clients with pro bono lawyers for civil law problems, including housing, fines, and administrative law. Justice Connect also supports foreign nationals through its online legal self-help tools and referral system.

For foreign visitors unsure where to turn, the best place to start is either a Community Legal Centre in their area or the Legal Aid Commission in the state where they are located. The Law Society in each state also maintains directories of lawyers who offer low-cost or pro bono services. Even if a visitor is not eligible for ongoing legal representation, they can often access free consultations or initial legal guidance through these services.

Foreign Embassies in Australia

Foreign embassies in Australia serve as official diplomatic missions that represent their home countries and provide support to their citizens while abroad. Nearly every country with diplomatic relations with Australia has an embassy, high commission, or consulate located in the country. These embassies play a key role in maintaining bilateral relations, issuing visas, handling diplomatic affairs, and offering consular assistance to their nationals.

As of 2025, there are approximately **112 foreign embassies and high commissions** officially accredited to Australia, the majority of which are located in **Canberra**, the national capital. These diplomatic missions represent countries from every continent and serve both diplomatic and consular roles. In addition to these embassies and high commissions, there are also over **300 consulates and honorary consulates** spread across major cities like **Sydney, Melbourne, Brisbane, Perth,** and **Adelaide,** where large numbers of foreign nationals live, work, or study.

Most foreign embassies are concentrated in the **suburb of Yarralumla** in Canberra, a district that serves as the core of the diplomatic community. This location is close to Parliament House and other key government institutions, making it strategically important for diplomatic engagement.

Countries with the **most extensive diplomatic representation** in Australia tend to be those with strong economic, political, or migration ties to Australia. These include:

- The **United States**, which maintains a large embassy in Canberra and consulates in Sydney, Melbourne, Perth, and other cities.
- The **United Kingdom**, with a high commission in Canberra and consulates in major cities, reflecting deep historical and Commonwealth ties.
- **China**, which has an embassy in Canberra and multiple consulates, including in Sydney, Melbourne, and Perth, reflecting significant trade and immigration links.
- **India**, with a high commission in Canberra and consulates in Sydney, Melbourne, Perth, and Brisbane, due to a large and growing Indian-Australian population.
- **Indonesia**, Australia's closest Asian neighbor, which maintains an embassy and several consulates across the country.
- **Japan**, **Germany**, **France**, **New Zealand**, **Canada**, and **South Korea** also have strong representation, reflecting robust bilateral relationships and large expatriate or student communities.

These countries not only maintain embassies and high commissions, but also operate **multiple consulates-general** and **honorary consulates**, offering services across different regions to their nationals and to Australians seeking visas or business connections.

The presence and spread of diplomatic missions reflect both the scale of international engagement with Australia and the needs of foreign nationals living or traveling there.

For a full list of all foreign missions, their addresses, and contact information, the official Department of Foreign Affairs and Trade directory is available at

https://www.dfat.gov.au/about-us/foreign-embassies/foreign-embassies-and-consulates-in-australia.

MEDICAL FACILITIES & HOSPITALS

MEDICAL FACILITIES & HOSPITALS

Overview

Australia's healthcare system is **widely regarded as one of the best in the world**, known for its comprehensive coverage, high standards of care, and combination of public and private services. It consistently ranks highly in global health system comparisons for quality, efficiency, and outcomes.

The healthcare system operates through a dual model: the **publicly funded Medicare system** and a robust private healthcare sector. Medicare, established in 1984, provides all Australian citizens and permanent residents with access to free or subsidized treatment by health professionals such as doctors, specialists, and public hospital services. It is funded through general taxation and a Medicare levy (currently 2% of taxable income). Individuals can also choose to purchase **private health insurance**, which offers faster access to elective surgeries, a broader choice of specialists, and coverage for services not included under Medicare, like dental and optical care.

In terms of accessibility, the system strives for **universal coverage**, but rural and remote communities sometimes face challenges due to doctor shortages and long travel distances. To address this, the government supports **telehealth**, **rural incentive programs**, and **mobile clinics**. Most Australians have relatively easy access to general practitioners (GPs) and emergency services, although wait times for certain specialists and elective surgeries in the public system can be long.

The **quality of care** is **generally high** across both the public and private sectors. Hospitals are well-regulated, and healthcare professionals are highly trained. Preventive care, maternal and child health services, mental health support, and chronic disease management are areas where Australia performs particularly well.

Affordability is where Australia shines in contrast to many other countries. **Public hospital care is free** under Medicare, and most **GP visits** are bulk billed, meaning there is **no out-of-pocket cost**. However, patients using private hospitals or services outside Medicare may face significant expenses unless covered by insurance. Prescription medications are subsidized under the **Pharmaceutical Benefits Scheme** (**PBS**), making many essential drugs affordable.

For emergencies, Australia has a nationwide number: **000** (triple zero), which can be dialed for police, fire, or ambulance services. For non-emergency health issues, Australians can call **13 HEALTH (13 43 25 84)** in most states, a 24/7 helpline staffed by registered nurses who provide health advice and guidance.

Visitors' Access to Healthcare in Australia

Visitors to Australia can access medical services, but the availability and cost of care depend heavily on their visa type, nationality, and insurance status. Unlike citizens and permanent residents, **visitors are not eligible for Medicare unless they are from a country that has a Reciprocal Health Care Agreement (RHCA) with Australia.**

Countries with RHCAs include the **United Kingdom, New Zealand, Ireland, Sweden, the Netherlands, Finland, Norway, Belgium, Slovenia, Italy,** and **Malta.**[31] Visitors from these nations can receive some

---

31 https://www.servicesaustralia.gov.au/
    about-reciprocal-health-care-agreements?context=22481

medically necessary care through Medicare, typically limited to emergency treatment or urgent care for pre-existing conditions. However, this **coverage is temporary and limited in scope**. It does not usually include ambulance services, dental work, or elective procedures. For all other visitors, medical care must be paid out of pocket unless they have travel or international health insurance.

Travel insurance is strongly recommended for all tourists and short-term visa holders. Without it, hospital care can be very expensive—often thousands of dollars per day for emergency treatment in public hospitals. Even a visit to a general practitioner (GP) can cost around $60 to $100 USD if not bulk-billed or subsidized.

Language barriers can be a concern, especially for visitors who do not speak English fluently. However, Australia has **extensive language support services**. The Translating and Interpreting Service (TIS National) is a free, government-funded service available 24/7 for non-English speakers, providing interpreters over the phone or in person during medical consultations. Hospitals and many clinics routinely use TIS to help ensure patients can understand medical advice, consent to treatment, and communicate symptoms effectively.

Australian Hospitals

Australia's healthcare system is supported by a **well-established hospital network** that combines both public and private facilities. As of 2023–24, there are **672 public hospitals** across the country providing admitted patient care services. These are government-funded institutions offering free or subsidized healthcare under Medicare, often handling emergency cases, major surgeries, and specialist care. By July 2024, there were also **647 private hospitals** in operation, offering more than 36,000 beds and playing a vital role in elective procedures, maternity services, and shorter wait times for non-urgent surgeries.[32] Altogether,

---

32 https://www.health.gov.au/sites/default/files/2024-11/private-hospital-financial-viability-health-check-summary.pdf

this brings the total number of hospitals in Australia to approximately 1,319.

Hospitals are primarily concentrated in major metropolitan areas such as **Sydney**, **Melbourne**, **Brisbane**, **Perth**, and **Adelaide**, where most of the population resides. These urban centers are home to some of the country's top hospitals. Public hospitals like the **Royal Melbourne Hospital**, **Royal Prince Alfred Hospital** in Sydney, and **Royal Brisbane** and **Women's Hospital** are nationally recognized for excellence in trauma care, cancer treatment, and research. In the private sector, hospitals such as **Epworth HealthCare** in Melbourne and **Sydney Adventist Hospital**—often referred to as "The San"—consistently rank among the best for high-quality patient care and advanced surgical services.

For international visitors, medical care is readily available but not covered under Australia's public Medicare system unless the visitor is from a country with a Reciprocal Health Care Agreement. Private hospitals such as **The Wesley Hospital** in Brisbane and **Epworth** have specific services to accommodate international patients, offering support with language services, care coordination, and travel documentation. However, travel health insurance is strongly recommended, as hospital treatment can be expensive for non-residents.

There is no specific American hospital operating in Australia today, although during World War II the U.S. Army ran the 118th General Hospital in Sydney, which was the largest American military hospital in the country at the time. Currently, no medical institutions are affiliated with American hospital networks.

Insurance Guidance

Foreign insurance plans are **not automatically accepted** by Australian hospitals or clinics. In most cases, visitors must **pay out of pocket first** and then submit claims to their overseas insurer for reimbursement. Some private hospitals or doctors may accept **direct billing arrangements** with major international insurers like Allianz Worldwide or Bupa Global, but this is not guaranteed and should be confirmed in advance.

Medical costs in Australia can be high for uninsured visitors. A **visit to a general practitioner** (**GP**) can cost between **$60 and $100 USD** depending on location and whether the provider bulk-bills. A **specialist consultation** typically ranges from **$120 to $250 USD**. An **emergency room visit** can cost **$300 to $600 USD** without admission. If hospitalization is required, daily inpatient fees can exceed **$1,000 USD** per day, especially in private hospitals.

Visitors are expected to **pay at the time of service**, usually by **credit card or EFTPOS** (**debit**). Larger hospitals may also accept bank transfers or international payment platforms. It is advisable for travelers to keep all receipts and medical records to facilitate reimbursement through their insurance provider later.

In short, visitors should not assume their foreign insurance will be accepted at the point of care. To avoid steep bills, it's best to **purchase comprehensive travel insurance** that covers medical emergencies, hospitalization, and repatriation, and check whether their plan offers cashless access or reimbursement options for providers in Australia.

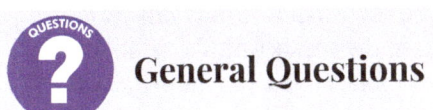 **General Questions**

1. *What number do I call in a medical emergency in Australia?*
   In a medical emergency in Australia, you should call **000** (**triple zero**).

   This is the national emergency number and connects you to **ambulance**, **police**, or **fire services**. The call is free from any phone, including mobile phones without credit. When you call, you'll be asked whether you need **ambulance**, **police**, or **fire**, and then be connected to the appropriate service. For **non-emergency medical advice**, most states also offer 24/7 health hotlines. For example, in Queensland, you can call **13 HEALTH** (**13 43 25 84**) to speak with a registered nurse.

2. ***Will I be treated if I don't have insurance?* Yes.** You will be treated in a medical emergency even if you don't have insurance. Australian public hospitals provide emergency care to everyone, including visitors. However, if you're not covered by Medicare or a reciprocal health agreement, you'll be billed in full for all services. Emergency room visits, ambulance transport, and hospital stays can be very expensive, often costing hundreds to thousands of dollars. This is why the government strongly recommends travel insurance for all visitors.

3. ***Should I go to a public or private hospital?*** As a visitor, you can go to either a public or private hospital in Australia, but the choice depends on your situation. For emergencies, public hospitals are the better option—they're widely available, well-equipped, and required to treat you regardless of insurance status. Private hospitals offer faster service and more comfort, but they usually require upfront payment or proof of international insurance. If your condition isn't urgent and you have travel insurance, a private hospital might be more convenient.

4. ***Do I need to pay upfront for medical treatment?*** In most cases, **yes**—you will need to pay upfront for medical treatment in Australia if you're a visitor. Public hospitals may bill you after emergency care, but many clinics, private hospitals, and specialists require payment at the time of service. You can usually pay by credit card or EFTPOS, and then seek reimbursement from your travel insurance provider later. If your insurance has a direct billing arrangement with the provider, upfront payment may not be necessary, but this is not guaranteed.

5. ***What if I need a prescription in Australia?*** If you need a prescription in Australia, you'll first need to see a local doctor—either at a general practice or hospital—to get one, even if you were prescribed the medication in your home country. Not all international prescriptions are accepted, so a local consultation is required. Once prescribed, you can fill the medication at any pharmacy, known locally as a "chemist." You'll need to pay for the medicine upfront, as visitors aren't eligible for Australia's government subsidy (the PBS), unless covered by a reciprocal

agreement. Keep receipts to claim through travel insurance if your plan covers prescriptions.

6. *Can I bring my medication to Australia?* **Yes.** You can bring your medication to Australia, but there are strict rules. You should carry only a personal supply, usually up to a three-month amount, and keep it in its original packaging with your name clearly labeled. It's also important to bring a copy of your prescription or a letter from your doctor explaining why you need the medication. Declaring all medicines at customs is essential to avoid fines or confiscation.

7. *What should I do in case of a medical emergency while traveling in Australia?* If you experience a medical emergency while traveling in Australia, call **000** immediately to request an ambulance. This is the national emergency number and is free from all phones. Emergency services will take you to the nearest public hospital for treatment. If you're able, carry your passport, travel insurance information, and any medical documents with you. After receiving care, you'll likely need to pay the bill unless you're covered by a reciprocal health agreement or have valid travel insurance. Be sure to keep all receipts and medical records for insurance claims. If you're in a remote area, local medical clinics or flying doctor services may provide emergency care until you can reach a hospital.

CHAPTER 18

DRIVING IN AUSTRALIA

DRIVING IN AUSTRALIA

Overview

Driving in Australia offers a generally smooth and enjoyable experience, especially for those exploring the country's diverse regions. In cities like Sydney, Melbourne, and Brisbane, roads are well-maintained and traffic systems are modern. Highways along the east coast are developed and easy to navigate, while roads in the Outback or remote areas can be unsealed, narrow, and occasionally affected by extreme weather. Travelers should be prepared for long distances without services in some rural regions, and for wildlife such as kangaroos crossing the road, especially around dawn and dusk.

Foreign drivers can legally operate a vehicle using their **home country license if it's in English**. If not, an **International Driving Permit (IDP)** must accompany the original license. Some states may require both documents regardless of language. Compulsory Third Party (CTP) insurance is required by law and is usually included in vehicle registration or rental fees. For those renting a car, it's wise to confirm whether additional comprehensive insurance is included or should be purchased separately to cover damage or theft.

Australian road customs include **driving on the left side** and using right-hand drive vehicles. Traffic laws are strictly enforced, and speed cameras are common. Roundabouts require drivers to yield to the right and signal when exiting. In Melbourne, a unique road feature called the

hook turn requires vehicles to turn right from the left lane in certain intersections—this can be confusing for first-time visitors. U-turns are only permitted where signs indicate, and **overtaking is done on the right**, with slower vehicles often pulling into the shoulder on rural roads to allow passing.

Toll roads operate in major urban areas and are **completely cashless**. Local drivers typically use **electronic tags** like Linkt, while tourists can either register their rental car or personal vehicle online for temporary passes. These can be set up before traveling or shortly after using the toll road, and payments can be made through websites like **Linkt.com.au**.

Rental companies may also bill tolls automatically with an added administrative fee, so it's important to check their toll policy in advance.

Overall, driving in Australia is straightforward for foreign visitors who understand local rules, have proper documentation, and are prepared for rural conditions. With some planning, it's an excellent way to experience the country's vast and varied landscapes.

 ## Main Traffic Rules

- **Driving Side:** In Australia, people drive on the left side of the road, and vehicles have the steering wheel on the right.

- **Speed Limits:** Speed limits are usually posted in kilometers per hour (km/h). Typical limits are 50 km/h (31 mph) in urban areas, 100–110 km/h (62–68 mph) on highways, and 40 km/h (25 mph) in school zones during certain hours.

- **Traffic Signals:** Traffic lights follow a red–amber–green system, similar to many Western countries. Left turns on red are not allowed unless clearly signed. Roundabouts are common, and drivers must yield to vehicles on their right.

- **Seat Belts:** Seat belts are mandatory for all passengers, and fines apply if anyone is caught without one. Child restraints are required based on age and size.

- **Alcohol:** The legal blood alcohol limit is 0.05% for full license holders. For learners and provisional drivers, the limit is zero. Random breath testing is frequent, especially on weekends and holidays.

- **Mobile Devices:** It is illegal to use a hand-held phone while driving. This includes texting, calling, or using GPS. Hands-free devices are allowed, but full attention must remain on the road.

- **Toll Roads:** Toll roads are cashless and mostly found in major cities like Sydney, Melbourne, and Brisbane. Visitors can set up a temporary pass online (e.g., via Linkt) or toll charges may be billed through rental car agencies.

- **If Stopped by Police:** Stay calm, remain in the vehicle, and follow instructions. Police may ask for your driver's license, IDP (if required), and vehicle documents. You may be asked to take a breath test.

- **Road Safety:** Australian roads are generally safe, but hazards like wildlife, long distances, extreme heat, and unsealed roads in rural areas pose risks. Always carry water, rest regularly, and plan routes carefully when traveling in remote areas.

 ## General Questions

1. *Can I use my driver's license from my home country to drive in Australia?* **Yes**. You can use your driver's license from your home country to drive in Australia **if it is in English** and you are a **temporary visitor**. If your license is **not in English**, you must carry an **International Driving Permit** (**IDP**) along with your original license. Some states may require both documents even

177

if your license is in English. If you plan to stay longer than three months, check local state or territory rules—some may require you to apply for an Australian license.

2. ***What is the age requirement for renting a car in Australia?***
The minimum age to rent a car in Australia is typically **21 years old**, but this can vary by rental company. Most companies require drivers to have held a **full driver's license for at least 12 months.** Drivers **under 25 may** face **young driver surcharges** and may be restricted from renting certain vehicle types. Always check the rental company's specific age and license policies before booking.

 ## Law of the Land Hypothetical

HYPOTHETICAL: *Jasmine, a 26-year-old visitor from Canada, is touring Australia for a month. She holds a valid Canadian driver's license, which is in English, and rents a car to drive from Sydney to Melbourne. While passing through a toll road near Sydney, she doesn't notice any toll booths and assumes she can pay later. Is Jasmine legally responsible for toll charges and the extra administrative fee, even if she didn't know the toll road was cashless?*

ANSWER: *Yes. Jasmine is legally responsible for paying both the toll charges and the administrative fee. In Australia, most toll roads are completely **cashless**, meaning there are no physical toll booths. It is the driver's responsibility to either set up a **temporary electronic toll pass** or ensure the rental company handles toll payments. Rental agreements often state that tolls will be charged automatically to the credit card on file, along with an administrative fee for processing. Not knowing the system does not exempt her from the charges, and the rental company is within its rights to collect both the toll and the fee. Travelers should always confirm toll policies when renting a car in Australia.*

NUDE BEACHES & CLOTHING-OPTIONAL RESORTS

NUDE BEACHES & CLOTHING-OPTIONAL RESORTS

Overview

In Australia, nudism's legality **depends on the state and specific location**. In parts of Australia—especially coastal regions and designated areas—nudity is culturally accepted, and there is a well-established nudist culture supported by local naturist communities. However, nudism is **not permitted in public places unless officially designated**.

There are several **legal nude beaches** throughout the country. These include famous spots like **Lady Bay Beach** in Sydney, **Maslin Beach** in South Australia (the country's first official nude beach), **Sunnyside North Beach** in Victoria, and **Alexandria Bay** in Queensland's Noosa National Park. These beaches are clearly signposted as clothing-optional or nudist-friendly and are regularly visited by both locals and tourists who practice naturism.

In addition to public beaches, Australia also has **nudist resorts and accommodations** that cater to naturists. Some popular examples include **River Island Nature Retreat** in New South Wales, **Tindo Naturist Resort** in South Australia, and **Secluded Glades** in Queensland. These resorts offer private, clothing-optional environments with facilities such as pools, camping areas, and communal spaces specifically designed for naturist lifestyles.

While public nudity outside of designated areas can result in fines or legal issues, naturism within approved spaces is legally protected and socially accepted in those contexts.

Legality and Safety

Nudism in Australia is regulated mainly through **state and territory laws** concerning **public decency, indecent exposure, and offensive behavior,** with specific allowances for designated nude beaches and private naturist clubs. Each jurisdiction sets its own rules about where nudity is legal, and penalties for public nudity outside approved areas can include fines or even criminal charges.

In **New South Wales**, public nudity is **generally illegal** except in certain approved locations like **Lady Bay Beach** near Sydney. Local councils and police enforce regulations based on the **Summary Offences Act,** which prohibits offensive behavior or indecent exposure in public places unless at designated clothing-optional zones.

Victoria also **restricts public nudity,** but allows it on designated nude beaches such as **Sunnyside North Beach.** The Summary Offences Act makes it illegal to be naked in public places unless authorized, so nudism is confined to official areas or private property.

In **Queensland**, the laws are stricter. The **Public Nuisance Act** and local council regulations **generally prohibit public nudity** except within private clubs or resorts. There are few officially designated nude beaches, so public nudity can lead to fines or legal action.

South Australia has more **formal recognition of nudism**, notably with **Maslin Beach** as the first official nude beach. The Summary Offences Act regulates offensive behavior, but authorities generally tolerate nudity within designated zones.

In the **Australian Capital Territory** and **Northern Territory**, public nudity is **largely prohibited** except on private land or in private clubs. The law is enforced under public decency or offensive conduct provisions, and there are **no officially sanctioned nude beaches.**

Western Australia prohibits public nudity under **laws related to offensive behavior**, but some remote beaches are informally tolerated for naturism. Official nude beaches are rare, and enforcement is stricter in populated areas.

Tasmania follows similar rules, restricting nudity to private property or designated beaches. Public nudity elsewhere can result in penalties under the **Police Offences Act**.

Nevertheless, across all states and territories, private naturist clubs and resorts do operate legally, providing safe spaces for nudism. Visitors are advised to familiarize themselves with local laws before engaging in nudism to avoid fines or legal trouble.

Safety concerns related to nudism in Australia are generally low when practiced in designated areas, but there are a few important issues to be aware of. One concern is **privacy and unwanted attention**. Although nudist beaches and resorts are intended to be respectful spaces, there have been occasional reports of voyeurism, inappropriate behavior, or people taking photos without consent. Most designated nude beaches are patrolled or have signs warning against such behavior, and offenders can be removed or reported to authorities.

Another concern is **sun exposure**. Australia has one of the highest rates of skin cancer in the world, so sunburn is a major risk—especially when nude. Sunscreen should be applied generously and frequently, and shade should be used when available. **Insect bites** and **dehydration** can also be concerns, especially in remote coastal areas, so carrying water and bug repellent is advised.

As for **nudist etiquette**, there are a few key guidelines that are widely respected in naturist communities:

- **Respect personal space:** Don't stare or behave in a way that makes others uncomfortable. Nudist areas are non-sexual environments.
- **Photography is not allowed:** Never take photos or videos without clear, explicit permission. Most nudist beaches strictly forbid photography.

- **Sit on a towel:** It's standard practice and good hygiene to sit on a towel when using public seating, picnic areas, or shared surfaces.

- **Follow signage and boundaries:** Only be nude in clearly marked clothing-optional areas. Being nude outside of those zones can be illegal.

- **Avoid sexual behavior:** Naturist spaces are about body freedom and comfort, not sexual expression. Any inappropriate conduct can lead to police involvement or bans from certain locations.

- **Be discreet when arriving and leaving:** Cover up when walking to and from nudist areas unless you're on private property where nudity is allowed.

Following these norms helps ensure that nudist spaces remain safe, legal, and welcoming for everyone.

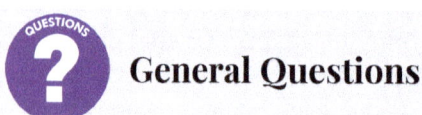 **General Questions**

1. *Are there clear laws protecting nudity on designated nude beaches, or can enforcement vary depending on local councils or police discretion?* **Yes.** There are laws in place that allow nudity on designated nude beaches, but enforcement can vary by state and even by local council. In most cases, these beaches are clearly signposted as clothing-optional and are protected under state or local government regulations. However, outside of these approved zones, public nudity is generally illegal and can lead to fines or legal action. Even within designated areas, police or rangers have the authority to intervene if someone's behavior is considered offensive or inappropriate, so it's important to follow proper nudist etiquette.

2. *What should I do if I witness inappropriate behavior or feel unsafe while visiting a clothing-optional beach in Australia?* If you witness inappropriate behavior or feel unsafe at a nude beach, it's recommended to leave the area and report the

incident. Many nude beaches are patrolled occasionally by park rangers or local authorities, and signs often include contact numbers for reporting misconduct. If immediate help is needed, you can call the local police using **000**, the emergency number in Australia. Naturist communities and advocacy groups also encourage reporting problematic behavior to help protect the respectful, non-sexual environment that these beaches are meant to provide.

 ## Law of the Land Hypothetical

HYPOTHETICAL: *Daniel, a backpacker from Germany, visits Maslin Beach in South Australia, which he reads is an official nude beach. While relaxing nude on the sand, he takes a few selfies and some panoramic shots of the beach, unknowingly capturing other sunbathers in the background. A nearby couple sees him taking photos and reports him to a park ranger. Can Daniel face legal consequences for taking photos at a designated nude beach, even if he didn't intend to photograph anyone else?*

ANSWER: *Yes. Daniel could face legal consequences or be asked to leave the beach. While Maslin Beach is a designated clothing-optional area, privacy and consent are taken very seriously in naturist environments. Most nude beaches in Australia have clear rules or signs prohibiting photography, regardless of intent, to protect visitors from voyeurism or unintentional exposure. Taking photos without explicit permission from everyone captured—even in the background—can be seen as a violation of privacy and may be considered offensive behavior under public decency laws. Even if no charges are filed, authorities can confiscate images or request deletion, and repeated violations could lead to fines or bans from public spaces. Visitors to nudist areas should avoid taking any photos to ensure respect for others' privacy and to remain within the law.*

UNUSUAL LAWS

UNUSUAL LAWS

Overview

Unusual laws can be fascinating glimpses into a culture's values and history. While most people are aware of common legal restrictions, it's often the strange and quirky laws that capture our attention. These regulations can range from the amusing to the absurd, reflecting the unique circumstances and traditions of a place. Whether they arise from historical events, societal norms, or simply peculiar local customs, unusual laws can provide insight into the quirks of human behavior and governance.

 **Unusual Australian Laws and Associated Penalties**

Australia is known for its laid-back culture, but it also has some unique and quirky laws—many of which are still enforceable and can carry surprising penalties. Here are a few examples:

- In **Western Australia**, it's illegal to possess more than 50 kilograms (about 110 pounds) of potatoes if you're not a licensed grower or seller under the Marketing of Potatoes Act. While the law is rarely enforced today, the maximum fine historically could reach **AUD**

$2,000 (about **$1,320 USD**) for a first offense and **AUD $5,000** (roughly **$3,300 USD**) for subsequent ones.

- In **Victoria**, it's illegal to change a light bulb unless you are a licensed electrician. This comes from an outdated interpretation of safety regulations. Although rarely enforced today, violating electrical safety laws could theoretically lead to a **fine of up to AUD $10,000** (around **$6,600 USD**), depending on the circumstances.

- In **Queensland**, singing an obscene song in public is prohibited under the Summary Offences Act. This includes lyrics deemed offensive or indecent. If charged, you could face a **fine of up to AUD $100** (about **$66 USD**) or even short-term imprisonment.

- In **South Australia**, it's illegal to disrupt a wedding or funeral under the Summary Offences Act. Doing so can result in a **fine of up to AUD $10,000** (approximately **$6,600 USD**) or two years' imprisonment.

- In **New South Wales**, under the Restricted Premises Act, it is illegal to have more than one unregistered vacuum cleaner in your home if it's believed you're running an unlicensed business. While this law is mostly symbolic and seldom enforced, potential penalties could include **seizure of the equipment** or **fines exceeding AUD $500** (roughly **$330 USD**).

Although many of these laws are obscure or outdated, they are technically still in force, and breaking them—even unintentionally—can sometimes result in surprising legal consequences.

 **General Questions**

1. *How strictly are outdated laws, like needing a licensed electrician to change a light bulb in Victoria, actually enforced?*
   Outdated laws like requiring a licensed electrician to change a

light bulb in Victoria are rarely, if ever, actively enforced today. They remain on the books mostly for safety reasons, but typical everyday actions like changing your own light bulb generally won't lead to penalties. Enforcement tends to focus on serious electrical work rather than minor tasks.

2. *How do quirky or outdated laws in Australia affect everyday life for locals, and are people generally aware of them?* Quirky or outdated laws in Australia generally have little impact on everyday life for most locals. Many of these laws date back decades and remain on the books without active enforcement, so people often aren't fully aware of them or simply ignore them. For example, few would seriously worry about rules like needing a licensed electrician to change a light bulb or limits on potato possession, because these laws are rarely applied in modern contexts. That said, some quirky laws do occasionally come up in legal or social discussions, often as curiosities rather than serious issues. Most Australians focus on current, practical regulations, but the old laws can sometimes be cited humorously or used to highlight how legal systems evolve over time. Overall, while these laws exist, they rarely affect daily behavior or cause legal problems for locals.

 ## Law of the Land Hypothetical

HYPOTHETICAL: *Emma, a tourist from Europe, visits South Australia and decides to fly a kite on a busy public promenade. Some local pedestrians complain that the kite is annoying and distracting them. A local officer approaches Emma. Is Emma breaking the law by flying a kite in public and can she be fined for it in South Australia?*

ANSWER: *Yes. In some Australian states, including South Australia, laws exist that prohibit activities like flying kites or causing a public nuisance if it annoys or disturbs others. While such laws are rarely enforced strictly, Emma could theoretically be fined if her kite flying is deemed disruptive under local public nuisance regulations. The fines might not be very high but are intended to keep public spaces safe and pleasant for everyone. Tourists should be mindful of their surroundings and avoid activities that could bother others, even if they seem harmless.*

CHAPTER 21
TRAVELING SAFELY

TRAVELING SAFELY

Ladies Traveling Solo

Australia has a strong reputation for being a safe and welcoming destination for travelers, including those exploring the country on their own. It consistently ranks **among the safest countries globally**, thanks to its low crime rates, political stability, reliable public services, and overall quality of life.

As such, Australia is generally considered very safe for women traveling alone. Solo female travelers frequently report feeling comfortable and secure in most parts of the country, especially in well-populated cities like Sydney, Melbourne, Brisbane, and Perth.

That said, there are **some areas where extra caution is advised.** Remote outback regions, while stunning and culturally rich, can pose risks due to their isolation, extreme temperatures, and limited access to emergency services. If venturing into the outback, it's important to travel with a plan, plenty of water, a reliable vehicle, and a way to communicate. In urban areas, **certain nightlife districts** like Kings Cross in Sydney, Fortitude Valley in Brisbane, and Northbridge in Perth can become rowdy late at night, especially on weekends. While violent crime is rare, incidents involving alcohol or petty theft can occur, so it's wise to stay alert and avoid walking alone in poorly lit or unfamiliar areas.

For solo female travelers, taking **common-sense safety precautions** can make a big difference. Staying in well-reviewed accommodations, avoiding hitchhiking, keeping your phone charged, and trusting your instincts are all key. It's also important not to leave drinks unattended, use lockers in hostels for valuables, and let someone know your travel plans—especially if heading into rural or remote regions. While mobile coverage is strong in cities and towns, it can be spotty in remote areas, so a backup battery and offline maps can be useful. Remember the emergency number in Australia is **000**.

Overall, Australia is an excellent and safe destination for women traveling solo. With its friendly locals, well-developed infrastructure, and culture of outdoor adventure, it offers a great balance of comfort and excitement, provided that basic precautions are taken.

Traveling as a Family

Traveling to Australia with children can be an unforgettable and enriching experience. The country is extremely family-friendly, with a wide range of kid-focused activities, clean facilities, and excellent public infrastructure. That said, a bit of preparation can make the journey smoother and safer for families.

One of the most important things is planning around Australia's vast size. Destinations can be far apart, and long drives or flights might be tiring for young children. Focus on a few regions rather than trying to see the whole country in one trip. Cities like Sydney, Melbourne, and Brisbane have excellent family attractions, while coastal areas like the Gold Coast or Cairns offer nature, wildlife, and adventure in a more relaxed setting. If you're visiting the outback or remote locations, make sure to plan fuel stops, pack extra water, and let someone know your route in advance.

Pack for the weather and sun—Australia's UV levels are among the highest in the world. Children should **wear sunscreen, wide-brimmed hats**, and **protective clothing**, and they need to **drink plenty of water throughout the day**. Consider bringing lightweight strollers with sun covers and insect netting, especially if you'll be spending time outdoors. In tropical and bushland areas, insect repellent and long sleeves help protect against bites. It's also a good idea to carry a small first-aid kit, including antiseptic cream, bandages, and children's medications like pain relief or allergy medicine. Pharmacies are widely available, but having essentials on hand is helpful if you're on the road or in a rural area.

Australia is home to some of the world's most iconic and potentially dangerous wildlife, including **sharks, crocodiles, and other marine creatures.** While this might sound intimidating, actual incidents are extremely rare, and Australia takes extensive precautions to protect both locals and tourists—especially families. Shark attacks are very uncommon, and the risk is minimal if you follow local advice. Most popular beaches have shark nets and are patrolled by lifeguards who monitor conditions closely. Always swim between the red and yellow flags, which mark safe zones. Avoid swimming at dawn or dusk when sharks are more active, and never swim alone or in areas with signs warning of shark sightings.

Crocodiles are found in **northern parts of Australia**, particularly in Queensland, the Northern Territory, and northern Western Australia. These include both freshwater and the more aggressive saltwater crocodiles. Crocodile attacks are rare but can be deadly, so **it's critical to obey all warning signs** near rivers, estuaries, and coastal waters. Do not let children play near the water's edge in crocodile-prone areas and never swim in places where crocodile sightings have been reported. Many safe and croc-free swimming areas are available, including man-made lagoons in cities like Cairns and Darwin.

Australia also has marine stingers like **box jellyfish** and **Irukandji**, mostly found in northern waters during the warmer months (roughly November to May). During this time, beaches will often have stinger nets, and wearing protective stinger suits—available for rent at beaches and tour companies—is strongly recommended for anyone entering the ocean, including children.

Teach kids to **observe animals from a distance** and **never touch or feed them**. Follow posted warnings in national parks and nature reserves. At beaches, only **swim at patrolled areas** between red and yellow flags, and **consider stinger suits** in northern regions during marine stinger season. If visiting crocodile-prone areas in the north, follow signage strictly, stay away from the water's edge, and always keep children close.

Food in Australia is **diverse, high-quality**, and **generally very safe to eat**. Thanks to its multicultural population, Australia offers a wide variety of cuisines—from traditional British and Irish comfort foods to vibrant Asian, Mediterranean, and Middle Eastern dishes. Cities like Sydney and Melbourne are especially known for their world-class dining scenes, where you'll find everything from budget-friendly street food to award-winning fine dining.

For families, food is usually easy and convenient. Most restaurants and cafes are child-friendly, with kids' menus, high chairs, and casual atmospheres. Supermarkets like Woolworths, Coles, and Aldi carry a wide selection of familiar international brands as well as fresh produce, ready meals, and baby food. Australian tap water is clean and safe to drink across the country, which helps cut down on bottled water costs and makes food preparation simple.

Health and hygiene standards are high, so foodborne illnesses are uncommon. Local specialties include **meat pies, sausage rolls**, "brekkie" staples like avocado toast and flat whites, and **seafood** such as barramundi, prawns, and Moreton Bay bugs. You'll also find **strong coffee culture** and plenty of vegetarian, vegan, gluten-free, and allergy-conscious options, especially in urban areas.

For children, the food is generally mild and approachable, and even picky eaters will likely find something they enjoy—like chicken schnitzel, pasta, fresh fruit, or toasted sandwiches ("toasties"). Many restaurants cater to dietary needs and are used to accommodating families and travelers.

Finally, **travel insurance is highly recommended for families** traveling to Australia. While Australia has excellent healthcare, it can be expensive for visitors, especially those who are not covered by a reciprocal health care agreement. Travel insurance helps protect your family against unexpected medical costs, trip cancellations, lost luggage, and other emergencies.

Do's and Don'ts While in Australia

Australia is known for its relaxed and friendly culture, but like any country, it has its own social norms and expectations. Here are some general cultural do's and don'ts to keep in mind while visiting:

DO'S:

- **Do respect Indigenous culture and heritage:** Always ask before taking photos on Aboriginal land or at cultural sites. Some areas are sacred and may be off-limits to tourists.

- **Do obey all wildlife and environmental rules:** Australia takes conservation seriously. Stick to designated paths, don't feed or approach wild animals, and follow posted signs—especially in national parks and marine areas.

- **Do follow road rules carefully:** Drive on the left side of the road, wear seat belts, and avoid using your phone while driving. Speed and traffic cameras are common and strictly enforced.

- **Do be sun smart:** Australia has one of the highest UV levels in the world. Wear sunscreen, a hat, and sunglasses—even on cloudy days.

- **Do greet people politely:** A simple "Hello," "Hi," or "How's it going?" is a normal and friendly way to start a conversation. Australians tend to be informal, but respectful.

- **Do tip—if service is exceptional:** Tipping is not mandatory, but appreciated for good service, especially in restaurants. Around 10% is considered generous.

- **Do dispose of trash properly:** Littering is not only frowned upon, it can also earn you a fine. Recycling is also taken seriously.

- **Do be honest and straightforward:** Aussies value authenticity and directness. It's fine to speak plainly—as long as you're respectful.

DON'TS:

- **Don't brag or act superior:** Australians generally dislike arrogance and appreciate humility. "Tall poppy syndrome" refers to the cultural tendency to cut down those who seem boastful.

- **Don't assume everyone's the same:** Australia is multicultural, with people from many ethnic and religious backgrounds. Be open and respectful of different lifestyles.

- **Don't compare everything to your home country:** Constantly saying how things are "better back home" can come off as rude.

- **Don't talk politics or religion unless invited:** These topics can be sensitive, and Australians often prefer to keep such conversations light unless they know you well.

- **Don't take offense to jokes:** Aussie humor can be sarcastic, blunt, or teasing, but it's rarely meant to be hurtful. It's often a sign of friendliness.

TOURIST TAXATION

TOURIST TAXATION

Overview

Tourism is a significant contributor to the Australian GDP. In 2023-24, tourism GDP was $78.1 billion, representing 2.9% of the total Australian economy.[33] This is a substantial amount, demonstrating the importance of tourism to the national economy. It supports a wide range of industries such as hospitality, transportation, retail, and entertainment, creating millions of jobs across both urban and regional areas. Many rural communities rely heavily on tourism for economic development and infrastructure investment. Additionally, international visitors bring in foreign currency, which helps improve Australia's trade balance and strengthen the Australian dollar. Tourism also encourages growth in related sectors like agriculture, construction, and cultural industries, making it a key driver of broader economic activity.

Tourists visiting Australia are required to pay certain taxes to help support the country's infrastructure and services that both visitors and locals rely on. The taxes help fund things like transportation, security at borders, maintenance of tourist sites, and overall public facilities. By paying these taxes, tourists help ensure that Australia can provide a safe, enjoyable, and well-maintained experience for everyone who travels there.

---

33 https://www.tra.gov.au/en/economic-analysis/tourism-satellite-accounts/national-tourism-satellite-account

Tourist Taxes in Australia

The main tax included in most purchases by tourists in Australia is called the **Goods and Services Tax** (**GST**), embedded in the prices of goods and services they buy during their stay. This means that the cost you see for shopping, dining, or accommodations already includes applicable taxes. For international travelers, there is also a **Passenger Movement Charge** (**PMC**), a departure charge included in the price of your airline or cruise ticket, which helps cover border security and customs services. Some local areas may add extra accommodation levies, and certain natural parks or attractions charge fees to support conservation efforts.

The taxes on purchases are calculated as a percentage of the price and are included automatically, so you don't usually need to pay them separately at the time of purchase. The departure charge is a fixed amount per passenger and is collected by your airline or cruise line when you buy your ticket. If you buy goods above a certain value during your trip, you may be eligible to claim **a refund on the taxes** paid for those items when you leave Australia by presenting receipts and the goods at the airport or seaport.

Tourists in Australia may be eligible for **a tax refund** through the **Tourist Refund Scheme** (**TRS**), which allows them to claim back the Goods and Services Tax (GST) on certain purchases made during their stay. To qualify, travelers must have spent at least AUD $300 (including GST) at a single retailer with the same Australian Business Number (ABN) within 60 days before departing Australia. They must also be taking the goods with them as part of their carry-on or checked luggage when leaving the country.

To claim the refund, tourists must present their **original tax invoices**, the **goods**, **their passport**, and **boarding pass** at the TRS facility located at international airports or seaports. If the items are oversized or restricted (like liquids or aerosols), they must be shown to Australian Border Force staff before check-in. Refunds can be paid via credit card, Australian bank account, or mailed cheque.[34]

---

34 https://www.abf.gov.au/entering-and-leaving-australia/
    tourist-refund-scheme

Tourists can speed up the process by using the TRS mobile or web app before arriving at the airport. However, they still need to present the physical goods and documents in person. If tourists bring these goods back into Australia on a future visit and exceed the duty-free allowance (AUD $900, or about $594 USD for adults, and AUD $450, or about $297 USD, for children), they may be required to repay the refunded tax.

There are a few additional points tourists should keep in mind about taxation in Australia. First, while most taxes like the Goods and Services Tax (GST) are included in the prices of goods and services, **not all expenses are eligible for a refund**—items like food, accommodation, and services (such as tours or haircuts) generally do not qualify under the Tourist Refund Scheme.

Tourists should also be aware that refunds are **only available when departing from Australia's international airports or seaports**, and the claim must be made within the airport's TRS facility before departure.

Another important detail is that the **refund applies only to physical goods carried in your luggage**—anything shipped or sent by mail won't qualify. Also, if you're part of a group or family, each person must make their own TRS claim unless all purchases are made under one name and that person is present during the claim. If you plan to return to Australia, and the total value of refunded goods exceeds the duty-free limit, you may need to declare them and potentially repay the refunded GST upon re-entry.

Finally, since some local councils are pushing for regional tourism levies (like accommodation taxes), it's a good idea to check if the place you're visiting charges additional fees on hotel stays. These may not be covered by national rules but could still appear on your final bill.

 **Law of the Land Hypothetical**

HYPOTHETICAL: *Elena, a tourist from Spain, spent two weeks traveling through Australia. Before flying home from Sydney, she purchased over AUD $500 worth of designer clothing from a major department store. She saved all her original receipts and planned to claim a GST refund through the Tourist Refund Scheme (TRS). At the airport, however, she checked in her luggage before visiting the TRS counter and realized the clothing was now in her checked baggage, which she could no longer access. Can Elena legally claim a GST refund under the Tourist Refund Scheme if the goods are in her checked luggage and not available for inspection at the TRS counter?*

ANSWER: ***No***. *Under current Australian law, Elena* **cannot** *claim the GST refund unless the goods are physically presented at the TRS facility before departure. According to the Australian Border Force, travelers must show both the goods and the original tax invoices when making a claim. If the items are packed in checked luggage that has already been processed, and cannot be presented for inspection, the refund will not be granted. To be eligible, Elena should have visited the TRS counter before checking in her bags, or packed the goods in her carry-on luggage.*

CHAPTER 23

LONG-TERM STAYS

CHAPTER 23

LONG-TERM STAYS

Overview

Many people choose to live in Australia long-term for its high quality of life, stable economy, and healthy, outdoor lifestyle. With a unique blend of modern cities, iconic beaches, and natural wonders, the country appeals to a wide range of people—from retirees and professionals to international students and young families. Australia is known for its **multicultural society**, **low crime rate**, **clean cities**, and **robust infrastructure**, making it one of the most livable countries in the world.

Popular long-term destinations include **Sydney**, **Melbourne**, and **Brisbane**, each offering a vibrant city lifestyle with cultural events, job opportunities, and top-tier amenities. Coastal cities like **Gold Coast** and **Perth** provide a more relaxed, beach-oriented way of life, while inland cities such as **Canberra** and **Adelaide** tend to be quieter and more affordable. Whether you're looking for excitement, calm, or a bit of both, Australia offers diverse options for long-term living.

Australia is considered a **relatively high-cost country**, though this is balanced by high wages and public services. **Sydney** and **Melbourne** are the most expensive cities. Rent for a one-bedroom apartment in the city center can range from **$2,700 AUD to $4,000 AUD ($1,800 USD to $2,700 USD)**. In smaller or less expensive cities like **Adelaide** or **Hobart**, you might pay around **$1,800 AUD to $2,400 AUD ($1,200 to $1,600 USD)** per month.

A meal at a mid-range restaurant would typically cost **$40 AUD to $60 AUD** ($27 USD to $40 USD), while monthly public transport passes in major cities cost around **$150 AUD to $190** (**$100 USD to $130 USD**). Groceries and services are high quality, but many expats find Australia's prices steep compared to Southern Europe or Southeast Asia.

Healthcare Options

As discussed in Chapter 17, Australia has one of the best healthcare systems in the world. The attractiveness of Australia's healthcare system to foreign visitors lies in its **high quality**, **modern facilities**, and **affordability** compared to countries like the U.S. Public healthcare is available to residents and eligible long-term visa holders through **Medicare**, and private insurance is widely used to access faster care and more choices. Even private medical services are often **less expensive than in many Western countries**, making Australia appealing for those concerned about medical costs during extended stays. The system is known for being **safe**, **efficient**, and **well-regulated**, which reassures visitors seeking reliable care abroad.

Housing Options

Housing in Australia is diverse and depends heavily on location, lifestyle, and budget. Major cities like **Sydney** and **Melbourne** tend to have higher housing costs, with a focus on **apartments**, **townhouses**, and **inner-city living**. These areas are popular for their convenience, public transport access, and job opportunities, but they come with premium prices. In smaller cities like **Adelaide**, **Canberra**, or **Hobart**, housing is generally **more affordable** and spacious, making them attractive to families or those looking for a quieter lifestyle. **Suburban areas** across the country offer larger homes with yards, while **regional towns** provide a more relaxed pace of life and lower property costs.

Most long-term residents begin by **renting**, especially while they're getting settled. Rental agreements are typically straightforward, and furnished or unfurnished options are available. Over time, some residents choose to **buy property**, with Australia offering a stable real estate market, though there are restrictions for foreign buyers without permanent residency.

Transportation Options

Australia offers a wide range of transportation options that make it relatively easy for visitors and long-term residents to get around. In major cities like **Sydney**, **Melbourne**, **Brisbane**, and **Perth**, public transportation is **well-developed**, **safe**, and **efficient**. Visitors can use **buses**, **trains**, **trams**, and even **ferries** to navigate urban areas without the need for a personal vehicle. Most cities have reusable transit cards (like **Opal** in Sydney or **Myki** in Melbourne) that make it easy to hop between different modes of transport.

For those staying primarily in cities, **owning a car is not necessary**. Public transit is generally reliable, and many neighborhoods are walkable with access to shops, restaurants, and services. **Taxis**, **rideshares**, and bike or scooter rentals are also widely available for shorter trips.

However, in **regional or rural areas**, public transport is much more limited. If you plan to live or travel outside the main cities—or want to explore more remote parts of the country—a **car becomes essential**. Roads are generally in excellent condition, and Australia is well-suited to road trips, though visitors should remember that **Australians drive on the left side** of the road.

For longer-distance travel between cities or states, **domestic flights** are fast and relatively affordable, while **long-distance buses and trains** offer scenic alternatives for those not in a rush.

Language Considerations

Australia's official language is **English**, making it easy for most Americans, Brits, and Canadians to settle in. That said, expats may need to adjust to **local slang**, **accents**, and **cultural norms**, which vary by region. The country is extremely multicultural, and many Australians speak a second language at home, especially in major cities. For non-native English speakers, numerous language schools and TAFE institutions offer **English classes** for all levels. While it's entirely possible to live in Australia speaking only English, embracing the local expressions and style of communication helps with both integration and employment.

Long-Term Visas[35]

Australia offers several long-term visa options tailored to different purposes—work, study, family reunion, retirement, or skilled migration. Choosing the right one depends on your goals and eligibility.

- **Skilled Independent Visa (Subclass 189):** Designed for qualified individuals with in-demand occupations to live and work anywhere in Australia without sponsorship. Application fee: **$4,640 AUD ($3,060 USD)**. Processing time typically **6 to 12 months.**

- **Skilled Nominated Visa (Subclass 190):** Requires nomination by an Australian state or territory government. Similar to Subclass 189, with a fee of **$4,640 AUD ($3,060 USD)**. Processing time usually **6 to 12 months.**

- **Temporary Skill Shortage Visa (Subclass 482):** Employer-sponsored visa valid up to four years for workers filling labor shortages. Starting fee: $1,455 AUD ($960 USD), with variations for longer terms and dependents. Processing often **under six months.**

- **Student Visa (Subclass 500):** Allows full-time study and limited work rights. Application fee: **$710 AUD ($470 USD)**. Processing generally takes **1 to 3 months.**

- **Partner Visa (Subclass 820/801 or 309/100):** For those in genuine relationships with Australian citizens or permanent residents. Fee: **$8,850 AUD ($5,840 USD)**. Processing time can be **15 to 25 months.**

- **Investor Visa (Subclass 188):** For financially independent individuals willing to invest in Australia. Fees start at **$6,270 AUD ($4,140 USD)**. Processing times usually **12 months or more.**

---

35 https://www.thisisaustralia.com/visa-listing/#work-visas

To apply, all visa applications must be submitted online via the official immigration portal at **https://immi.homeaffairs.gov.au/help-support/tools/immiaccount.** Applicants must first create an **ImmiAccount**, then choose the appropriate visa type, complete the required forms, upload supporting documents, and pay the application fee. For some skilled or nominated visas, applicants are required to submit an **Expression of Interest** (**EOI**) through SkillSelect before applying. The entire process is digital, and communication from the Department of Home Affairs is generally managed through the online system.

Visa Application Requirements[36]

To apply for most Australian long-term visas, applicants typically need to meet several general requirements regardless of visa type. Applicants must have a **valid passport** from their country of citizenship. They usually need to provide **proof of identity and any relevant personal documentation** such as birth certificates or national ID cards. Most visas require applicants to submit **health examinations** conducted by approved doctors to ensure they meet Australia's health standards and do not pose a public health risk.

Character checks are mandatory; applicants often need to provide **police clearance** certificates from countries where they have lived for a significant time. This is to confirm they have no serious criminal history. Additionally, **proof of financial capacity** may be requested to demonstrate that applicants can support themselves and any dependents during their stay.

Depending on the visa, applicants might also need to provide **evidence related to their purpose of stay**, such as educational qualifications for student visas, skills assessments for skilled migration, sponsorship details for employer-nominated visas, or relationship evidence for partner visas.

---

36 https://usa.embassy.gov.au/visa-requirements

All applications require submitting **completed forms**, paying the appropriate **visa fee**, and often providing **biometrics** (fingerprints and photos) at designated centers. English language proficiency tests may also be necessary for certain skilled or professional visas.

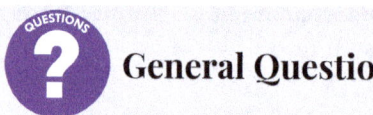

General Questions

1. *If I want to stay in Australia for long-term and work, should I apply for a work permit before arriving in Australia?*
   Yes. You must secure the appropriate Australian work visa before you arrive; there is no option to obtain a work permit on arrival. Visit the Department of Home Affairs website, choose the visa that matches your occupation and situation, complete the online application, satisfy health and character requirements, and wait for approval before traveling.

2. *I am American. Can I retire to Australia?* **Yes.** As an American, you can retire to Australia, but there's no dedicated retirement visa. Most retirees explore the Investor Visa (Subclass 188), which requires significant financial investment and business experience. Some also apply through family visas if they have close relatives in Australia. Bear in mind that all long-term options require meeting health, financial, and character requirements, and must be applied for before arrival.

Law of the Land Hypothetical

HYPOTHETICAL: *Emma, a 29-year-old graphic designer from the United States, receives a job offer from a digital marketing agency in Melbourne. The company is eager to have her start as soon as possible and suggests she come to Australia on a tourist visa while they sort out the paperwork for the Temporary Skill Shortage Visa (Subclass 482). Can Emma enter Australia on a tourist visa while her employer sponsors her for a Subclass 482 work visa?*

ANSWER: *No. Even though Emma can legally enter Australia on a tourist visa, she cannot begin working until her Subclass 482 visa is officially granted. Additionally, if her tourist visa includes the "no further stay" (Condition 8503) clause, she won't be able to apply for a different visa—like the Subclass 482—while in Australia. She would then need to leave the country and apply offshore. Even without that condition, Immigration may question her intentions if she enters as a tourist but clearly plans to stay and work. This could raise red flags or lead to delays in her future visa processing. It's strongly recommended that Emma wait until her Subclass 482 visa is approved before traveling to avoid complications or potential visa breaches.*

 **Takeaways**

- Australia offers multiple visa options for long-term stays, including skilled migration, employer sponsorship, student, partner, and investor visas—each with specific eligibility criteria and application procedures.

- Applying for visas requires meeting strict health, character, and financial requirements, including police background checks and in some cases, proof of English language proficiency or investment capacity.

- Visa applications must be completed before arrival, as Australia does not grant work or residency rights to tourists; applying from outside the country is usually required, especially if your current visa has a "no further stay" condition.

- There is no dedicated retirement visa, so retirees typically explore investor pathways or family sponsorship options if they wish to settle long-term in Australia.

- The cost of living varies widely by region, but in general, it is higher than in many countries. Cities like Sydney and Melbourne are more expensive, while smaller cities and regional areas offer more affordable housing and lifestyle options.

- Long-term residents have access to excellent healthcare, through Medicare (if eligible) or private insurance, with costs lower than in the U.S. but higher than in some European countries.

CIVIL LITIGATION

CIVIL LITIGATION

Overview

Civil litigation provides a mechanism for resolving disputes, ensuring that travelers have a way to seek justice if legal issues arise while visiting another country. It helps them understand their rights and obligations under local laws, which may differ from those in their home country. The civil litigation system offers a formal process for addressing conflicts, such as contract disputes or personal injury claims, and can deter unfair practices by encouraging businesses to comply with legal standards. It also allows individuals to seek financial recourse for damages or losses and helps protect them from potential exploitation by local entities. Overall, understanding civil litigation enhances a visitor's experience and safety while traveling.

Personal Injury Claims and Compensation Law

If you suffer a personal injury due to someone else's negligence—such as a car accident, slip and fall, or workplace incident—you may be entitled to **compensation** through the Australian legal system. Each state and territory has its own laws and processes, but generally, you can file a claim for medical expenses, loss of income, pain and suffering, and rehabilitation costs.

In most cases, injured parties first claim through **insurance schemes**. For motor vehicle accidents, **Compulsory Third Party (CTP) insurance** covers injury claims against the at-fault driver. For workplace injuries, workers' compensation schemes provide benefits and medical care. To make a claim, you usually need to prove the other party was at fault (negligent) and that this caused your injury. This process often involves medical assessments and legal advice. Claims must be filed within specific time limits (statutes of limitations), which vary by state but typically range from 1 to 3 years from the injury date.

Visitors to Australia can file personal injury claims, but they must act quickly, especially if they plan to return home. Legal representation is highly recommended to navigate the complexities of the system. Without compensation, injured persons are responsible for their own medical costs, which can be substantial. Therefore, many visitors are advised to have comprehensive travel insurance that covers personal injury and related expenses during their stay.

To file a personal injury claim in Australia, you should first **seek medical treatment** and **keep all related records and bills as evidence**. Next, **report the incident** to the relevant parties, such as the property owner, employer, or police, to officially document what happened. It's important to gather as much evidence as possible, including photos, witness contact details, and any communication related to the injury. Identify any insurance policies that may apply, such as motor vehicle Compulsory Third Party (CTP) insurance or travel insurance.

Consulting a **personal injury lawyer** who is familiar with the laws in the state or territory where the injury occurred is highly recommended. A lawyer can advise you on your rights, assess the strength of your claim, and guide you through the process. The claim will then be formally submitted to the responsible party's insurance company or the relevant compensation authority. Many cases are resolved through negotiation or mediation, but if necessary, the claim may proceed to court.

How to File a Civil Claim[37]

Filing a civil claim in Australia involves several important steps. To begin, you must ensure you meet the basic requirements, which generally include having a **valid legal cause for your claim**—such as breach of contract, negligence, or property damage—and identifying the correct defendant. The claim must be **filed within the applicable time limits** known as statutes of limitations, which vary depending on the type of claim and jurisdiction.

Civil claims can cover a wide range of issues, including personal injury, contract disputes, property damage, consumer complaints, and more. The specific type of claim you file will depend on the nature of your legal issue.

When preparing to file, you will need to gather key documents such as a completed claim form or statement of claim detailing your case, any relevant contracts or agreements, evidence supporting your claim (like photos or correspondence), and records of any attempts to resolve the matter before court.

The claim is typically **filed at the appropriate court or tribunal** based on the claim's value and subject matter. For smaller claims, this might be a local or Magistrates Court, while higher-value or more complex disputes go to District or Supreme Courts. Each state and territory has its own court system and filing procedures, so it's important to identify the correct venue, which is often where the defendant resides or where the dispute occurred.

Seeking legal advice can help ensure your claim is properly prepared and filed in the right place to increase the chances of a successful outcome.

---

37   https://courts.nsw.gov.au/resources/starting-or-responding-to-a-civil-claim.html

Service of Documents

In Australia, the service of legal documents is governed by the rules and procedures set out by the particular court or tribunal handling the matter. These rules vary slightly between jurisdictions, such as the Federal Court or various state courts, but generally share the same goal: ensuring that the party to whom the documents are addressed is properly and fairly notified of the legal proceedings. The service must be carried out in a manner consistent with these rules to avoid delays or the potential dismissal of the case due to improper notice.

Documents can be served through several methods. The most common and preferred approach is **personal service**, where the documents are delivered directly to the individual named. Alternatively, **service by post** is often used, employing registered or certified mail sent to the person's last known address. Service can also be made by **leaving documents at a residence or workplace with someone of suitable age and responsibility**. In some cases, if agreed upon or ordered by the court, documents may be served **electronically**, such as via email or fax. When these methods fail, the court may allow **substituted service**, which can involve alternative means like public notices or serving a representative of the person. Often, professional process servers or court bailiffs are engaged to ensure that service is performed correctly and in compliance with the law.

The responsibility for serving the documents usually lies with the plaintiff or their legal representatives, though they can appoint a process server or bailiff to carry out the task. The person serving the documents must be an adult who is not involved in the case. The process of service begins with preparing the documents according to court requirements, selecting the appropriate method of service, and then making the attempt to deliver the documents. Once service is completed, the person who served the papers must verify that the documents were properly delivered.

Proof of service is a **critical component in the process** and is documented through an affidavit or declaration sworn or affirmed by the individual who carried out the service. This document includes details such as the date, time, place, and manner of service, along with the identity of the person served or an explanation of substituted service. This affidavit is then filed with the court to demonstrate that the party has been duly notified. Without such proof, courts may refuse to proceed with the case until proper service is established. This framework ensures fairness in legal proceedings by guaranteeing that all parties have appropriate notice.

Statute of Limitations[38]

In Australia, the statute of limitations refers to the legally prescribed time limits within which a person must initiate legal proceedings for various types of claims. These time limits vary depending on the nature of the claim and the jurisdiction where the claim is made, as each Australian state and territory has its own legislation governing limitation periods. In Australia, statutes of limitations, while existing, are **primarily relevant in civil proceedings**. For criminal matters, there are no statutes of limitations for most serious offenses, but they do exist for certain summary offenses and some situations involving Commonwealth laws.

For **breach of contract** and **debt recovery** claims, the typical limitation period is **six years** from when the issue occurred, although in the Northern Territory this is reduced to three years. **Negligence claims** that do not involve personal injury also generally have a six-year limitation period, with the Northern Territory again having a shorter period of **three years. Defamation cases** must usually be brought **within one year** of the defamatory publication, but courts may extend this up to three years if justified. **Personal injury claims** typically have a **three-year limitation** period from the date the injury occurred or was discovered, with possible extensions in special circumstances. **Claims to recover land** usually have a much longer limitation period, commonly **12 years**, and in some jurisdictions, such as New South Wales, this may extend up to 30 years. The **enforcement of judgment debts** varies between states, typically ranging from **12 to 15 years**. These limitation

---

38 https://gibbswrightlawyers.com.au/publications/
limitation-periods-in-civil-proceedings/

periods can be subject to exceptions, including cases of fraud or where the claimant was under a disability, and the start of the limitation period can depend on when the cause of action was discovered. Missing these deadlines can prevent a claim from being heard, so it is important to seek legal advice promptly if you believe you have a claim.

There are exceptions to the statute of limitations in Australia where the limitation period may **be extended or "tolled,"** meaning the clock temporarily stops or is delayed from running. Common exceptions include situations involving **fraud or deliberate concealment**, where the defendant has hidden the cause of action or misled the claimant, preventing them from discovering the claim within the usual time limit. Another key exception applies when t**he claimant is a minor, legally incapacitated,** or **suffering from a disability** that affects their ability to take legal action; in these cases, the limitation period may be paused until the disability is removed or the claimant reaches the age of majority. Additionally, in some personal injury claims, the limitation period may begin only **when the injury is discovered**, not necessarily when it occurred, particularly for latent injuries that appear later. Courts also have some discretion to grant extensions of time if it is just and equitable, depending on the circumstances. These exceptions exist to ensure fairness and prevent injustice when strict adherence to limitation periods would unfairly bar legitimate claims.

 ## Getting Married in Australia

In Australia, getting married involves meeting specific legal requirements set out by the **Marriage Act 1961**. Both parties must be **at least 18 years old** to marry, although under exceptional circumstances, a court may grant permission for someone aged 16 or 17 to marry. Neither person can already be married, and the couple cannot be closely related. To apply for a marriage license, which in Australia is known as a **Notice of Intended Marriage** (**NOIM**), couples need to complete this notice at least **one month and no more than 18 months before the wedding date**. Required documents typically include **proof of**

identity such as birth certificates or passports, evidence of termination of any previous marriages (if applicable), and parental consent for those under 18 with court permission. **Foreign nationals can marry in Australia without any residency requirements**, but they must still comply with the same legal conditions.

The process for obtaining the NOIM involves completing the form with a registered marriage celebrant or at an Australian embassy or consulate if overseas. Once lodged, the celebrant will keep the form until the ceremony. Couples should allow at least one month for the notice period before marrying, though it is recommended to start earlier to allow for any complications. For civil ceremonies, the marriage must be conducted by a registered civil celebrant, while religious ceremonies are conducted by authorized religious ministers. Both types of ceremonies must comply with legal formalities, including the presence of witnesses and the signing of the marriage certificate.

After the ceremony, the marriage is registered with the relevant state or territory Registry of Births, Deaths and Marriages. The couple receives an official marriage certificate, which serves as proof of marriage. Generally, **Australian marriages are recognized overseas**, but couples planning to live abroad should verify recognition rules in the destination country, as requirements and formalities may differ. It is advisable to keep the official marriage certificate and any related documents safe for such purposes.

 ## Law of the Land Hypothetical

HYPOTHETICAL: *Liam, a tourist visiting Sydney, slips and falls on a wet floor inside a shopping mall. He suffers a broken wrist and incurs significant medical expenses during his stay. The mall management had failed to put up any warning signs about the wet floor. Can Liam file a personal injury claim in Australia to recover his medical expenses, and what important factors should he be aware of regarding timing and the claim process?*

ANSWER: *Yes. Liam can file a personal injury claim because the mall's negligence caused his injury. He must act quickly since personal injury claims typically have a three-year statute of limitations, but starting sooner is advisable. Liam should get medical treatment and keep all records, report the incident to mall management or their insurer, and gather evidence like photos and witness contacts. As a visitor with limited time, consulting a local personal injury lawyer is highly recommended to help file the claim with the mall's insurer and guide him through settlement or court processes if needed. Without a claim, Liam would bear his medical costs, so prompt action is important. He should also check that his travel insurance covers such claims while abroad.*

CHAPTER 25

OTHER THINGS TO KNOW

IN THIS CHAPTER

- Tourists and Street Hustling
- Safety Concerns and Practical Tips
- In the Event of Death
- Experiencing Financial Hardship

227

OTHER THINGS TO KNOW

Tourists and Street Hustling

Street hustling in Australia is **relatively mild compared to some other parts of the world**, but it does exist in certain tourist-heavy locations and can impact the experience of visitors who aren't aware of what to look out for. In most cases, street hustling in Australia takes the form of low-pressure interactions where individuals approach tourists to sell goods, ask for donations, or offer services. These encounters usually aren't aggressive, but they can be persistent or misleading. For instance, someone might pose as a struggling artist or charitable volunteer to solicit money, or hand out a "free" souvenir like a bracelet or postcard only to demand payment afterward.

The types of goods and services commonly offered by street hustlers range from cheaply made or counterfeit souvenirs to handmade jewelry that may not be as authentic as claimed. In some places, performers will dress up in costumes or offer photos with animals, then request a tip or fee afterward. Some people pose as club promoters offering free entry or tours, only for tourists to find out there are hidden costs involved later. A growing concern is the **sale of mass-produced Aboriginal art passed off as genuine**, which not only misleads tourists but also undermines real Indigenous artists.

Tourist-heavy cities like Sydney, Melbourne, the Gold Coast, and Cairns are where street hustling is most noticeable. In **Sydney**, spots like

Circular Quay, **Darling Harbour**, and **Bondi Beach** attract not just tourists but also people hoping to capitalize on them. In **Melbourne**, **Federation Square** and **Bourke Street Mall** are common zones for unsolicited sales or street pitches. On the **Gold Coast**, **Surfers Paradise** sees plenty of activity targeting young travelers and backpackers, while in **Cairns**, which is a gateway to the Great Barrier Reef, tourists may encounter club promoters and tour sellers who don't always deliver what they promise.

Several common scams stand out in these areas. One is the **"free gift"** trick, where someone gives a tourist a bracelet or souvenir and then insists on payment. Another involves people posing as **charity workers** with fake clipboards and IDs, collecting donations for causes that don't exist. Sometimes tourists are sold **tours or attraction tickets at a discount**, only to find out the experiences either don't exist or cost more than they were told. Artwork sold as **"authentic"** **Aboriginal pieces** may actually be imported and mass-produced, and unfortunately, many tourists are unaware they've been misled until much later.

Australian local governments take the issue seriously and enforce regulations around street vending and public solicitation. Many city councils require permits for street performers and vendors, and police regularly patrol high-traffic tourist areas to discourage scam behavior. Tourism organizations, including official websites like **Smartraveller**, also publish guidance for tourists to help them identify and avoid scams. In places like Sydney, licensing systems for performers help ensure that street activity is both legal and respectful of tourists' experiences.

For most tourists, street hustling in Australia is a **minor inconvenience rather than a threat**. Still, it can create discomfort or lead to financial loss if visitors aren't cautious. A little awareness goes a long way. Being prepared for how these scams typically work helps tourists enjoy their trip with confidence, knowing they can politely decline or walk away from suspicious encounters without worry.

Safety Concerns and Practical Tips

Safety concerns related to street hustlers in Australia are relatively **minimal** compared to high-risk destinations, but tourists should still **exercise basic caution**. The most common issues are petty scams that can lead to financial loss, as well as persistent or manipulative behavior that can make tourists feel uncomfortable or pressured. While physical aggression is rare, some hustlers may become verbally pushy if they sense a tourist is unsure or easily swayed. In crowded areas, distractions created by street performers or sellers can also make tourists more vulnerable to pickpocketing, although this is not widespread.

To stay safe, tourists should **avoid engaging with anyone who approaches them unsolicited** in the street, particularly those offering "free" items or collecting donations. It's best to keep wallets and phones secure, especially in crowded public places. Tourists should **trust their instincts**—if an interaction feels off or uncomfortable, walking away confidently is the best response. Maintaining a **polite but firm "no thanks"** and avoiding eye contact can help minimize engagement. It's also a good idea not to display large amounts of cash or expensive accessories, as this can signal vulnerability or wealth to opportunists.

Understanding local customs can also help tourists avoid awkward or unsafe encounters. Australians are generally laid-back and non-intrusive, so aggressive street solicitation is not part of the cultural norm. Most legitimate fundraising or public activity happens through regulated channels. If someone is being unusually persistent or emotional, it's likely a red flag. Being assertive without being confrontational is key—Australians respect directness, and a simple "I'm not interested" is typically enough to end the interaction.

If tourists do feel harassed, threatened, or believe they've been scammed, there are several resources available. Local police are accessible and responsive in most cities, and tourists can report incidents at nearby stations or call emergency services at **000**. Non-emergency matters can be directed to local police assistance lines. Many cities also have tourist assistance centers or local council hotlines for reporting scams or suspicious activity.

 Additionally, the **Australian Competition and Consumer Commission** (**ACCC**) provides information on scams and has an online reporting tool at **www.scamwatch.gov.au**.

Tourists can also reach out to their embassy or consulate for support, especially if identification, money, or travel documents are involved.

By staying aware, knowing what's normal, and using common sense, tourists can enjoy their time in Australia with confidence, minimizing the chances of falling victim to scams or uncomfortable street encounters.

 In the Event of Death

If someone traveling with you dies while in Australia, it's important to stay calm and follow the necessary legal and procedural steps to ensure the situation is handled respectfully and correctly. The first action is to **immediately contact local emergency services** by dialing **000** to report the death. If the person dies in a hospital or medical facility, the staff will handle the necessary notifications and documentation. In the case of sudden or accidental death, the police will get involved, and a coroner may be required to investigate and determine the cause.

Once authorities are notified, your next step is to **contact your home country's embassy or consulate** in Australia. They can help guide you through the process, including identifying the deceased, notifying next of kin, and coordinating with local officials. While the consulate will not cover costs, however they can provide a list of local funeral directors experienced in international repatriation, assist with legal documentation, and help communicate with authorities or insurance providers.

Handling the deceased's remains in Australia involves several formal steps. The death must be **officially registered** with the local state or territory registry of births, deaths, and marriages. Once that is complete, a **death certificate is issued**, which will be required for any further arrangements. The family then chooses either a burial or cremation in Australia or repatriation of the body to the home country. If the body is to be transported internationally, embalming is typically required, and the funeral director will handle permits, air transport arrangements, and coordination with international mortuary services.

For families bringing the body home, it's important to know that the process can be expensive and time-consuming, often costing between $5,000 and $15,000 USD or more, depending on the country of destination. Having **travel insurance that includes repatriation coverage** can significantly ease the financial and logistical burden. Documentation such as the death certificate, embalming certificate, and a "non-contagious disease" certificate will be needed for air transport. The embassy or consulate can assist in ensuring the required paperwork is correct and recognized by both Australian and international authorities.

Dealing with a death abroad is difficult, but Australia has a clear and compassionate process to help families manage these sensitive matters. By contacting local authorities and your consulate promptly, and working with licensed funeral providers, you can ensure the process is handled respectfully and legally.

Experiencing Financial Hardship

Experiencing financial hardship while traveling in Australia is not uncommon, especially given the country's high cost of living. Tourists may face money issues due to unexpected expenses like medical emergencies, theft, overspending, or poor budgeting. In some cases, flight cancellations, natural disasters, or losing access to bank cards can also create sudden financial stress. Backpackers and students on limited budgets are particularly vulnerable, especially in major cities where accommodation, transportation, and food can quickly add up.

If a tourist runs out of money or finds themselves in a financial emergency, the first step should be to **contact their home country's embassy or consulate**. While they won't provide direct cash assistance, they can help contact family or friends, facilitate wire transfers, and in extreme cases offer guidance on temporary accommodations or emergency loans arranged through the tourist's government. Tourists should also **notify their bank immediately** if their cards are lost, stolen, or frozen. Many international banks have partner branches in Australia, and some can issue replacement cards or cash advances.

There are **limited formal support systems** for financially distressed travelers, but certain **charities or church-based services** may provide short-term help like meals or shelter. Additionally, tourists in dire need may consider reaching out to their country's expat or cultural communities for help via social media or consulate referrals. Some travelers seek short-term work through platforms like **Workaway** or **HelpX**, where they can receive food and accommodation in exchange for labor, although these arrangements **must comply with visa conditions**.

Understanding the local currency and cost structure can help prevent these situations. Australia uses the Australian dollar (AUD), and exchange rates can fluctuate, impacting the actual cost of travel. Everyday items such as food, transportation, and attractions are generally more expensive than in many other countries. For example, a basic lunch might cost $12–$20 USD, and a single night in a budget hotel can run between $60 and $100 USD. Knowing this in advance can help tourists set realistic expectations.

Smart budgeting is essential. Tourists should track expenses daily, use cost-saving apps, and opt for prepaid SIM cards, public transport passes, and free or low-cost attractions. Bringing more than one form of payment, including cash, credit/debit cards, and a secure digital wallet, can prevent problems if one method fails. Travel insurance with emergency assistance benefits is also strongly recommended.

By planning carefully and being aware of the resources available, tourists can reduce the risk of financial hardship and know what to do if unexpected money problems arise while in Australia.

QUICK REFERENCE GUIDE

- Quick Chapter References to Important Topics

QUICK REFERENCE GUIDE

Crime in Australia

Are there particular areas I should avoid as a tourist?

Yes. Australia is generally very safe for tourists, with low levels of violent crime. Most tourist areas—like Sydney's Circular Quay, Melbourne's city center, and Brisbane's South Bank—are well-patrolled and welcoming. However, visitors should use extra caution at night in spots like Kings Cross (Sydney), St Kilda (Melbourne), and Fortitude Valley (Brisbane), where alcohol-related incidents and petty theft can occur. Remote areas in the Northern Territory or parts of Western Australia may also see higher crime rates, but tourists are rarely targeted. Staying aware of your surroundings, avoiding poorly lit areas at night, and keeping valuables secure will help ensure a safe trip. *For more details, see Chapter 3.*

Drug Offenses

Is the possession of marijuana legal?

Marijuana possession is mostly illegal in Australia, except in the Australian Capital Territory (ACT), where adults can legally possess up to 50 grams and grow up to two plants per person for personal use. In all other states and territories, **recreational use is prohibited**, though small amounts may result in fines or diversion programs rather than criminal charges. **Medicinal cannabis is legal**

nationwide with a prescription, but driving with THC in your system remains illegal everywhere.

Is the possession of cocaine legal?

Cocaine possession is **illegal throughout Australia**, though the Australian Capital Territory (ACT) has decriminalized possession of small amounts (up to 1.5 grams) for personal use, with penalties typically limited to a fine or diversion program rather than criminal charges. In all other states and territories, possession remains a criminal offense, with fines, charges, and possible imprisonment depending on the amount and circumstances. Trafficking and possession of larger quantities carry severe penalties nationwide. *For more details, see Chapter 4.*

Alcohol-Related Offenses

What is the legal drinking age?

The legal drinking age in Australia is **18 years old**. This applies uniformly across all states and territories for purchasing and consuming alcohol in licensed venues. However, laws regarding underage drinking in private settings, such as homes, vary by jurisdiction. In some areas, individuals under 18 may legally consume alcohol at home if provided by a parent or guardian, while in others, only parents or guardians are permitted to supply alcohol to minors. It's important to be aware of and adhere to local laws to avoid legal issues.

What is the legal blood alcohol limit to drive?

In Australia, the legal blood alcohol concentration (BAC) limit for **fully licensed drivers is 0.05%**. However, stricter rules apply to **learner**, **provisional**, and **probationary drivers**, as well as drivers of heavy vehicles and public passenger vehicles, who must maintain a zero BAC of **0.00%**. *For more details, see Chapter 5.*

Firearm & Ammunition Offenses

Can I possess a gun?

In Australia, tourists are **generally not allowed** to possess firearms unless they obtain a visitor's firearms license and necessary permits from the state or territory police **before** arrival. Importing or possessing a gun without proper authorization is a serious offense, punishable by heavy fines and imprisonment. Unauthorized possession or importation of firearms carries severe legal consequences.

Can I possess ammunition?

Tourists **cannot legally possess ammunition** without obtaining the proper permits and a visitor's firearms license from the relevant state or territory police **before** arrival. Ammunition possession is strictly regulated and linked to firearm laws. Unauthorized possession or importation of ammunition is a serious offense, carrying heavy fines and possible imprisonment. *For more details, see Chapter 6.*

Prostitution

Is prostitution legal?

Prostitution laws in Australia **vary by state**. In New South Wales, Victoria, Queensland, and the Northern Territory, sex work is **decriminalized** and regulated for health and safety. In South Australia, Western Australia, and Tasmania, many related activities like brothel operation and public solicitation remain **illegal**, making the industry more restricted. In the Australian Capital Territory sex work is **legalized** but requires brothels to be licensed and prohibits street solicitation. Laws differ widely, so it's important to know local regulations. *For more details, see Chapter 7.*

LGBTQ

Is homosexuality legal?

Yes. Homosexuality is **legal throughout Australia**. Same-sex sexual activity was decriminalized nationwide by 1997, and same-sex marriage has been legal since 2017. LGBTQ+ individuals are protected from discrimination under federal and state laws, making Australia one of the more LGBTQ+ friendly countries globally.

Are same-sex public displays of affection legal and socially acceptable?

Yes. Same-sex public displays of affection are generally accepted in major Australian cities like Sydney and Melbourne, where LGBTQ+ communities are strong and supportive. However, in regional or conservative areas, some may feel uncomfortable or unsafe showing affection publicly. While legal everywhere, it's wise to be aware of your surroundings and use discretion outside of more progressive urban centers. *For more details, see Chapter 8.*

Arrested in Australia

Would I be entitled to bail if I'm arrested?

Yes. If you're arrested in Australia, you are generally entitled to apply for bail. Bail allows you to be released from custody while awaiting trial, usually under certain conditions like reporting to police or surrendering your passport. However, bail isn't automatic—courts consider factors such as the seriousness of the offense, risk of fleeing, and public safety before granting it. The exact process and criteria can vary by state or territory.

Will a lawyer be provided to me if I cannot afford one?

If you're a tourist arrested in Australia and cannot afford a lawyer, **you may be eligible for legal aid, but this depends on the state or territory and the circumstances of your case.** Generally, legal aid is prioritized for residents and citizens, so tourists might face limitations. However, you have the right to request a lawyer and access to duty lawyers at police stations or courts, who can provide free initial advice and representation. It's important to ask for legal assistance immediately if arrested. *For more details, see Chapter 10.*

Helping a Friend or Relative Imprisoned in Australia

Can I send money to a friend or relative imprisoned in Australia?

Yes. You can send money to a friend or family member imprisoned in Australia, but rules vary by state and territory. Funds can be sent via bank cheque, money order, or electronic transfer—cash is usually not accepted. There are limits on how much money a prisoner can receive monthly, which differ depending on the location and security level.

Can I remain in the country upon release from prison or jail after my sentence is complete?

After completing a prison sentence in Australia, whether you can remain in the country **depends on your immigration status and the nature of your conviction**. If you are a tourist or non-citizen, Australian immigration authorities may cancel or refuse your visa due to your criminal record or prison sentence, which could lead to deportation. Permanent residents and citizens generally have the right to stay, but serious offenses might still affect their status. It's important to consult with an immigration lawyer to understand your specific situation. *For more details, see Chapter 12.*

Crime Victim Assistance

Can a victim of a crime be legally compensated?

Yes. As a tourist in Australia, you may be eligible for compensation if you're a victim of crime. Each state and territory administers its own compensation scheme, and many accept claims from foreign nationals. Eligibility typically requires reporting the incident to the police and providing supporting documentation, such as medical reports and evidence of financial loss. Application time limits generally range from two to three years, though extensions may be possible in certain circumstances. It's advisable to seek legal advice to navigate the process and understand your rights and options.

Does the Australian government offer assistance for family members of homicide victims?

> **Yes.** Australia offers financial assistance to family members of homicide victims, but the specifics vary by state. Eligibility and application processes differ, so it's best to contact local victim support services for guidance. *For more details, see Chapter 14.*

U.S. Consulate Assistance

Are there any limitations to the consulate assistance I can receive while in Australia?

> **Yes.** Consulate assistance while in Australia has some limitations. Consulates can help with emergencies like lost passports, legal advice referrals, and contacting family, but they cannot intervene in legal proceedings, pay your fines, or secure your release from jail. Their support is mostly administrative and advisory, so you remain responsible for following local laws and handling your own legal or financial issues. *For more details, see Chapter 14.*

Police

Is there an official police force?

> **Yes.** Australia has official police forces at both federal and state/territory levels. Each state and territory has its own police service responsible for law enforcement within their area, such as the New South Wales Police Force or Victoria Police. The Australian Federal Police handles national and cross-jurisdictional issues like organized crime and border protection. Together, they maintain public safety and enforce laws across the country. *For more details, see Chapter 15.*

How to Get Legal Help in Australia

Is there a resource in Australia to find legal representation?

Yes. Australia offers several resources to help find legal representation. Each state and territory has legal aid commissions that provide free or low-cost legal services to eligible people. Additionally, the Law Society or Bar Association in each region can offer referrals to qualified lawyers. Online directories and community legal centers also assist tourists and residents in finding the right legal help based on their needs.

Is there free legal representation assistance?

Yes. Tourists in Australia can sometimes access free or low-cost legal help through Legal Aid commissions and Community Legal Centres, but eligibility depends on factors like the type of case and visa status. Some services may be limited for visitor visa holders. It's a good idea to contact your country's consulate in Australia for guidance and to find local legal resources. *For more details, see Chapter 16.*

Foreign Embassies in Australia

Where can I find a complete and updated list of all diplomatic missions in Australia?

You can find a complete and updated list of diplomatic missions in Australia on the **Australian Government's Department of Foreign Affairs and Trade** website at **https://www.dfat.gov.au/about-us/foreign-embassies/foreign-embassies-and-consulates-in-australia**. This directory includes contact details and addresses for embassies and consulates.

Where is the U.S. Embassy in Australia located?

The U.S. Embassy in Australia is located in **Canberra** at Moonah Place, Yarralumla, ACT 2600. This embassy serves as the primary diplomatic mission of the United States to Australia and is one of the largest in the Australian capital. For more information or to contact the embassy, you can visit their official website: **https://au.usembassy.gov/**. *For more details, see Chapter 16.*

Medical Facilities & Hospitals

Is there a number I can call for ambulance and fire emergencies?

Yes. For ambulance and fire emergencies in Australia, call **000**, the national emergency number that connects you to police, fire, and ambulance services quickly.

If I am injured while on vacation in Australia, are there hospitals that are recommended for tourists?

Yes. If you are injured while on vacation, major cities like Sydney, Melbourne, and Brisbane have well-equipped public and private hospitals known for quality care, such as **Royal Prince Alfred Hospital** in Sydney and **The Alfred** in Melbourne. Many hospitals have experience treating tourists, but it's advisable to have travel insurance to cover medical costs. *For more details, see Chapter 17.*

Driving in Australia

Which side of the road do I drive on?

In Australia, you drive on the **left side** of the road.

Can I use my driver's license from my home country to drive in Australia?

Yes. You can usually use your valid driver's license from your home country to drive in Australia **for a limited time**, typically up to three months. It's recommended to also carry an official English translation or an International Driving Permit if your license is not in English.

How old do I need to be to rent a car?

The minimum age to rent a car in Australia is **generally 21 years old**, but some rental companies may require drivers to be 25 or older and may charge additional fees for younger drivers. *For more details, see Chapter 18.*

Nude Beaches & Clothing-Optional Resorts

Is public nudity legal on the beaches?

> **No.** Public nudity is not legal on most Australian beaches **unless** they are specifically designated as clothing-optional or nude beaches. At these approved locations—such as Maslin Beach in South Australia or Lady Bay Beach in Sydney—nudity is permitted. However, being nude on regular public beaches can lead to fines or legal consequences, so it's important to check local rules before disrobing. *For more details, see Chapter 19.*

Tourist Taxation

Is there room tax in Australia?

> **No.** There is no separate "room tax" in Australia like in some other countries. However, hotel stays include a 10% Goods and Services Tax (GST), which is already included in the advertised price.

Is there any fee associated with leaving Australia by air?

> **No.** There is no official departure tax for travelers leaving Australia by air. Any applicable Passenger Movement Charge (PMC) is typically included in the price of your airline ticket, so you won't need to pay it separately at the airport. *For more details, see Chapter 22.*

Long-Term Stays

Do I need to return to my home country to apply for a work permit in Australia?

> **Yes.** You cannot convert a tourist visa to a work permit while staying in Australia. By law, those on tourist visas are required to **leave Australia and apply from home** for a work visa. Some visas (like subclasses 417/462 for working holidays) must be applied for—and granted—**from outside Australia**, although certain partners or student visas may be eligible for onshore applications that allow a bridging visa while they're being processed .

As an American, how long can I stay in Australia without a visa?

As a U.S. citizen, you **cannot enter Australia without a visa**. The easiest option is the Electronic Travel Authority (ETA), which lets you stay **up to 90 days** per visit within a 12-month period. If you want to stay longer, you'll need to apply for a Visitor Visa (subclass 600). *For more details, see Chapter 23.*

In the Event of Death

What documents would an embassy need regarding the death of a tourist?

If a tourist dies in Australia, the embassy will typically need the deceased's full name, passport details, death certificate, cause of death (if known), next of kin contact information, and any available medical or police reports. These documents help the embassy assist with arrangements like repatriation, notifying family, and working with local authorities. *For more details, see Chapter 25.*

EMERGENCY/IMPORTANT CONTACT NUMBERS IN AUSTRALIA

 Please consider putting some of these numbers in your phone **prior** to traveling to Australia.

Emergency Numbers:

- **Emergency (Police, Fire, Ambulance):** 000
- **Mobile Emergency (GSM):** 112
- **Police Assistance (Non-Emergency):** 131 444
- **Healthdirect (Medical Advice):** 1800 022 222
- **Poison Information Centre:** 13 11 26
- **Lifeline (Mental Health Crisis):** 13 11 14
- **Beyond Blue (Mental Health Support):** 1300 22 4636
- **Kids Helpline:** 1800 55 1800
- **RSPCA (Animal Emergencies):** https://rspca-act.org.au/ contact-us

Other Useful Contacts:

- **Tourist Police:** No dedicated number; use 131 444 for non-emergency police assistance
- **Coast Guard (Marine Rescue):** 000 (for emergencies) or local Marine Rescue units – e.g., Marine Rescue NSW: 02 8071 4848
- **Roadside Assistance :** 13 11 11
- **National Relay Service (for hearing/speech impaired):** 1800 555 727

Legal Assistance:

- **Australian Bar Association:** +61 2 9229 1710
- **Legal Aid – National Referral:** 1300 888 529
- **Legal Aid NSW:** 1300 888 529
- **Victoria Legal Aid:** 1300 792 387
- **Legal Aid Queensland:** 1300 651 188
- **Legal Services Commission of South Australia:** 1300 366 424
- **Legal Aid Western Australia:** 1300 650 579
- **Legal Aid ACT:** 1300 654 314
- **Legal Aid Tasmania:** 1300 366 611
- **Community Legal Centres Australia (CLCs):** 02 9264 9595 or www.clcs.org.au

USEFUL AUSSIE SLANG PHRASES

"G'DAY!" – Hello

"HOW YA GOING?" – How are you?

"NO WORRIES!" – It's okay / You're welcome / Don't worry about it

"CHEERS!" – Thanks / Goodbye / Toast

"MATE" – Friend/Buddy (used casually for almost anyone)

"SHE'LL BE RIGHT" – Everything will be fine

"TOO EASY" – No problem / Happy to help

"BLOODY OATH!" – Definitely! / You bet!

"YEAH, NAH" – No (friendly way to decline)

"NAH, YEAH" – Yes (laid-back way to agree)

"FAIR DINKUM" – Genuine/True (e.g., "Is that fair dinkum?" = Is that legit?)

"FLAT OUT" – Really busy

"CHINWAG" – A casual chat

"BUGGERED" – Tired or worn out

"DODGY" – Suspicious or not trustworthy

"SHE'LL BE RIGHT" – It'll be fine / Don't stress

"STREWTH!" – Expression of surprise or disbelief

"FLAT OUT LIKE A LIZARD DRINKING" – Very busy

"HAVING A CHINWAG" – Having a chat

"SPIT THE DUMMY" – Throw a tantrum

"CHUCK A SICKIE" – Take a day off work by pretending to be sick

"GOING OFF" – Very busy, exciting, or wild (e.g., "That party was going off!")

GLOSSARY

ACQUITTAL: A jury verdict that a criminal defendant is not guilty, or the finding of a judge that the evidence cannot support a conviction.

ADVERSARY PROCEEDING: A lawsuit arising from a controversy that begins with filing a complaint.

AFFIDAVIT: A written statement made under oath.

APPEAL: A request made after a trial court has decided against one party in which the losing party asks a higher court to review the decision for legal error.

ARRAIGNMENT: A proceeding in which a criminal defendant is brought to court, told of the charges, and asked to plead guilty or not guilty.

BAIL: The temporary release of a person from jail when awaiting trial, on condition that a sum of money be lodged or deposited to guarantee an appearance in court.

BARRISTER: A lawyer admitted to plead at the Bar and who may try cases in superior court.

BURDEN OF PROOF: The duty to prove disputed facts.

CAUSE OF ACTION: A legal claim in a civil action.

COMPLAINT: A written statement that begins a civil lawsuit in which the plaintiff details the claims.

CONTRACT: An agreement between two or more persons to do something or to not do something.

CONVICTION: A judgment of guilt against a person charged with a crime.

CUSTOMS DUTY: A tariff or tax imposed on goods when transported across international borders.

COURT LIAISON: A person that coordinates with attorneys to perform administrative duties, such as scheduling witnesses, sharing information with law enforcement, and overseeing the reporting of cases to foreign embassies when applicable.

DAMAGES: Money that a defendant pays to a plaintiff in a civil case if the plaintiff wins.

DEFENDANT: 1) The individual against whom a civil claim is filed; 2) The individual against whom a criminal claim is filed.

FELONY: A serious crime, punishable by more than one year in prison.

MAGISTRATE: A judicial officer of a district court, who conducts initial proceedings in criminal cases, decides criminal misdemeanor cases, conducts many pretrial civil and criminal matters on behalf of district judges, and decides civil cases with the consent of the parties.

MISDEMEANOR: An offense punishable by one year or less in jail.

PLAINTIFF: A person or business that files a formal complaint with the court.

PLEA: In a criminal case, the answer of "guilty," "not guilty," or "no contest" in response to a criminal charge.

SOLICITOR: A lawyer who advises clients, represents them in lower court, and prepares cases for barristers to try in higher courts.

SOVEREIGN IMMUNITY: A legal doctrine by which the sovereign or the state (i.e. government) cannot commit a legal wrong and thus, it is immune from criminal and civil liability and cannot be sued.

STATUTE: A written law passed by a legislative body.

STATUTE OF LIMITATIONS: A statute prescribing a period of limitation to bring certain types of legal actions. If the action is not brought within that time, the person or entity (in a criminal context) is permanently barred from suing in court.

SUBPOENA: A command, issued under court authority, for a witness to appear and to give testimony.

TESTIMONY: Evidence presented orally by witnesses.

VERDICT: The decision of a judge or jury in a case.

WARRANT: Court authorization to conduct a search or to make an arrest.

ACKNOWLEDGMENTS

This book series would never have seen the light of day without the able assistance of the following people:

Kathy Adams, my paralegal for over 22 years, who is the "Best" I've ever worked with during my entire legal career because of her amazing work ethic, organizational skills, and her ability to think outside of the box in unique and creative ways;

Ally Knez-Siddique, a professional writer, and one of my paralegals, whose eye for detail, according to her, is both a blessing and a curse;

Gino Ibanez, my former law clerk, whose exceptional research skills helped move this book along in its early stages;

Rosa Diaz Graham, my legal assistant who helped with research and word processing at the very beginning of this project;

Shelia Martin, one of my former paralegals, worked diligently on this series of books, even after taking on another job. Her organizational skills are reflected throughout;

Mindy Scarlett, my marketing and publishing "Guru"! Her creativity and vision have no boundaries!

ABOUT THE AUTHOR

Michael L. Moore practices in Orlando, Florida, the city where he spent his formative years. He credits the trauma of having his brother murdered when he was only 10 years old, as the catalyst that drew him into the practice of law.

Moore attended Florida State University, where he was a member of the FSU debate team. Upon graduating, he was awarded a full scholarship to attend the University of Tennessee College of Law, where he was elected President of the Student Bar Association. He further honed his advocacy and public speaking skills by participating in 'moot court' competitions.

After clerking at the Tennessee Attorney General's office while in law school, Moore moved back to Orlando, Florida, to work at the State Attorney's Office as a prosecutor, and where he was fortunate enough to meet the young lady that would eventually become his wife. Moore moved on to working for private law firms, both local and national, and eventually established his own law firm in 1999. He continues to make Orlando his home base.

It was the murder of a close friend and client in Jamaica that caused Moore to realize that books on laws in other countries were few and far between, and he was inspired to create Law of the Land Publishing. Moore launched Law of the Land Publishing to provide a series of guidebooks and a membership site for tourists and business travelers to stay up to date on the laws in each country they travel to, as well as having access to assistance if they run into legal issues.

"My vision is to educate people on what their legal rights are, and how they can access legal assistance, no matter where they have to travel to in the world," said Moore. "As Americans, we have a right to due process, but in some countries, you don't even have the right to access a square meal when incarcerated. My goal is to provide the information needed to stay out of trouble, as well as having access to assistance if trouble finds you."